A TOUR TO THE FUTURE OF TOURISM

EMERGING CONCEPTS AND CONCERNS IN TOURISM

ANAGHA SATHEESAN T M

ISBN 979-888530930-1

"It is with genuine gratitude and warm regard that I dedicate this work to everything ,which is existing or existed in this globe........................... "

Anagha satheesan TM

Contents

Foreword

I am immensely pleased to present the first book written by Mrs. Anagha Satheesan TM, my student, and colleague who has taken a great effort, in order to make this book very useful. I assured that the readers would find it exciting and helpful. I appreciate the keen interest shown by Anagha in the academic and research arena of the tourism sector and am glad to introduce this book .

Smitha S

Head, Travel And Tourism Management

Providence women College, Calicut

Preface

"Travel is never a matter of money but of courage" – Paolo Coelho

Tourism is a known affair in human life. The theory and practice of touring, the business of attracting, accommodating, and entertaining tourists, and the business of operating tours are all the matters concerned in tourism. According to the United Nations World Tourism Organisation (UNWTO), tourism entails the movement of people to countries or places outside their usual environment for personal or business/professional purposes. Tourism, however long its incident duration, has become an extremely popular, global activity. . It has been an industry of vast dimensions and eventually supports economic and social growth. Tourism worldwide has experienced phenomenal growth. With more than 600 million people travelling annually, tourism is the world's largest industry, with revenues of about half a trillion dollars a year, and averaging five percent annual growth.

The tourism industry is one of the most resilient and dynamic sectors of the economy and will result in commensurate economic opportunities for developed and emerging destinations around the world. During 21th century tourism industry is characterized by numerous issues and trends that present threats and opportunities. Today, tour operators and tourists, both are equipped with the latest technology. It has empowered tourism business managers and tourists to explore, discover and reach new places by facilitating online travel and accommodation bookings, and more.

In this book, I attempt to cover the emerging trends in tourism, which have the great potential to shape the entire history in the upcoming future. Also, I try to address the growing concerns in the tourism industry as it was evolving day by day. The structure of the book has been designed to help readers get a systematic study of tourism. The approach has been to provide a simple and comprehensive outline of the subjects discussed. Howsoever no single book is sufficient to cover the subset in detail.

Anagha Satheesan TM

Acknowledgements

Gratitude is a quality similar to electricity: It must be produced and discharged and used up in order to exist at all. No duty is more urgent than that of returning thanks. I have a lot to be thankful to everyone who supports me, inspires me, lends their valuable time and effort to complete this book. writing a book is harder than I thought and more rewarding than I could have ever imagined.

Thank you ....

' GOD ' for blessing me much more than I deserve,

Achan n Amma for being the reason for my presence and Babi ettan for being the cause of my existence,

All the teachers who construct me, especially to DR Sr Ashmitha AC my beloved principal, Smitha mam, and Ann mam for your impeccable motivation and guidance,

Prasoon Ettan for being a great mentor,

My entire family and friends for standing behind me,

To my loving students who are the reason,

and finally from Herles-corona-Borealis Great wall to Quarks.......

Anagha Satheesan TM

CHAPTER ONE

THE SKY IS NOT THE LIMIT

*"I know the sky is not the limit because there are footprints on the Moon —
and I made some of them
~~-Buzz Aldrin*

SPACE TOURISM

Humans are explorers since before the dawn of civilization, we've been lured over the horizon to find food or more space, to make a profit, or just to see what's beyond those trees or mountains or oceans. Our capacity to investigate arrived at new statures. Our first steps into space began as a race between the United States and the former Soviet Union, rivals in a global struggle for power. On April 12, 1961, Yuri Gagarin (Russian Astronaut) travelled to space and stretched out his name forever in history. For the following forty years, space travel was only confined to astronauts.

In April 2001, Dennis Anthony Tito (born August 8, 1940) an American engineer and entrepreneur, became the first space tourist. He funds his trip into space, and he spent nearly eight days in orbit. Tito paid a reported $20 million for his trip. He was sent on a Russian Soyuz spacecraft. In April 2002, South African entrepreneur, Mark Shuttleworth became the second commercial space tourist, and Gregory Olsen in October 2005 became the third one in the lane.

Space tourism is human space travel for recreational purposes. There are several different types of space tourism, including orbital, suborbital, and lunar space tourism. A space tourist was the one who went to space spending his own money and could not be called a professional astronaut, so he was called a "touronaut". During the period from 2001 to 2009, seven space sightseers made eight space trips. The publicized price was in the range of US$20–25 million per trip. Some space tourists have signed contracts with third parties to conduct certain research activities while in orbit. By 2007, space tourism was thought to be one of the earliest markets that would emerge for commercial spaceflight. Several companies were planning to build suborbital vehicles and orbital destinations within the next two decades. These companies had invested millions, believing that the space tourism industry was on the verge of taking off.

TRAVEL TO OUTER SPACE

The space-age is now a half-century old. Over the past fifty years, since the launch of Sputnik, in October 1957 there have been remarkable achievements. For decades, the advancement in space technology and space exploration has been spearheaded by the official national space agencies.

The use of astronomy and space technology to explore outer space is known as space exploration. While astronomers use telescopes to explore space, physical exploration is done by both unmanned robotic space probes and human spaceflight.A "Space Race" between the Soviet Union and the United States propelled early space exploration. The launch of the Soviet Union's Sputnik 1, the first human-made object to orbit Earth, on 4 October 1957, and the first Moon landing by the American Apollo 11 mission on 20 July 1969 are often cited as watershed moments in this period.

Spaceflight (or space flight) is an application of astronautics to fly spacecraft into or through outer space, either with or without humans on board. Most spaceflight is uncrewed and conducted mainly with spacecraft such as satellites in orbit around Earth, but also includes space probes for flights beyond Earth orbit. Such spaceflight operates either by telerobotic or autonomous control.

In the 2000s, China initiated a successful manned spaceflight program when India launched Chandraayan 1, while the European Union and Japan have also planned future crewed space missions. China, Russia, and Japan have advocated crewed missions to the Moon during the 21st century, while the European Union has advocated manned missions to both the Moon and Mars during the 20th and 21st centuries. From the 1990s onwards, private interests began promoting space tourism and then public space exploration of the Moon

The National Space and Astronautics Administration (NASA) in the United States has made numerous strides.The European Space Agency (ESA), the French Space Agency (CNES), the German Space Agency (DLR), the Russian Space Agency (Roscosmos), the Japanese Space Exploration Agency (JAXA), the Chinese Space Agency, the Indian Space Research Organization (ISRO), the Brazil Space Agency (INPE) and other government space agencies have all made contributions. The US Space Shuttle and the Russian Soyuz programs have demonstrated that human access to space is possible with some regularity, and now true mass access to space appears to be on the horizon.

INTERNATIONAL SPACE STATION

The International Space Station is the most difficult scientific and technological project ever attempted. The International Space Station (ISS) is a modular (habitable artificial satellite) in low Earth orbit (is an Earth-centred orbit close to the planet). it is a multi-nation construction project that is the largest single structure, mankind has ever placed in space. The station's major construction took place between 1998 and 2011, however, it is constantly evolving to include new missions and experiments

According to the European Space Agency, the International Space Station is a "cooperative program" between Europe, the United States, Russia, Canada, and Japan. The station serves as a microgravity and space environment research laboratory in which scientific research is conducted in astrobiology, astronomy, meteorology, physics, and other fields. The ISS program evolved from the Space Station Freedom, an American proposal that was conceived in 1984 to construct a permanently manned Earth-orbiting station. The station is divided into two sections: the Russian Orbital Segment (ROS) is operated by Russia, while the United States Orbital Segment (USOS) is run by the United States as well as many other nations. The principal ISS part was dispatched in 1998, and the primary long-haul occupants showed up on 2 November 2000, the station has since been continuously occupied for 20 years. longest persistent human presence in low Earth circle. Originally, the ISS was intended to be a laboratory, observatory, and factory, while providing transportation, maintenance, and a low-Earth orbit readiness base for possible future missions to the moon, Mars, and asteroids.

Gravity at the height of the ISS is about 90% stronger than at the Earth's surface, but orbiting objects are in continuous free fall, resulting in an apparent state of weightlessness (Weightlessness is the complete or near-complete absence of the sensation of weight. This is also termed zero-G). The International Space Station (ISS) provides a safe environment in which to test spacecraft systems that will be required for long-duration missions to the Moon and Mars.

LUNAR TOURISM

The Moon is our closest celestial neighbour. Half a century ago, people made repeated visits. Lunar tourism may become a reality in the future if trips to the Moon are made available to a private audience. Some space tourism start-ups are proposing to offer tourism on or around the Moon, and believe that this will be possible between 2023 and 2043. Some space tourism start-ups have revealed how much a journey to the Moon will cost each traveller. Although this is merely a fly-by expedition and will not land on the Moon, Space Adventures is charging $150 million per seat, which includes months of ground-based training, Excalibur Almaz had the same price tag but never managed to send their capsule to space. The Golden Spike Company was planning to charge $750 million per seat for future lunar landing tourism. Two natural attractions would be available by circumlunar flight or lunar orbit, without landing View of the far side of the Moon and View of the Earth rising and setting against the lunar horizon. Space Adventures, Excalibur Almaz, Virgin Galactic, and SpaceX are among the space tourism companies that have indicated their interest in moon tourism.

DEAR MOON PROJECT

The dearMoon project is a lunar tourism mission, In 2023, a billionaire Japanese entrepreneur and a crew of eight artists and entertainers will embark on a mission that will take them "beyond what any human has left before" set to blast off inside a SpaceX Starship. The mission, known as dearMoon, is spearheaded by Yusaku Maezawa, who has paid an undisclosed sum to achieve his dream of going to the moon. He intended the dearMoon project to be something like a civilian art project.

The project was unveiled in September 2018 and the flight is expected to happen no earlier than 2023. The project's goal is to have six to eight passengers travel around the Moon for free on a six-day tour with Maezawa. Maezawa anticipates that the space tourism experience will inspire the accompanying passengers to create something new. The artwork would be displayed after they returned to Earth to help promote world peace. Yusaku Maezawa announced on March 3, 2021, that eight members of the public will be chosen to fly on dearMoon. He reveals 1 million people have joined, but there was still no information on who won the 8 seats. Maezawa didn't specify what qualifications are necessary to be selected for the mission, however, the dearMoon project requires candidates to screenings and interviews

SPACE TOURIST

1. Dennis Tito

Dennis Anthony Tito (born August 8, 1940) is an American engineer, entrepreneur, and astronaut. In mid-2001, he became the first space tourist to fund his trip into space, when he spent nearly eight days in orbit as a crew member of ISS EP-1, a visiting mission to the International Space Station. This mission was launched by the spacecraft Soyuz TM-3 2nd was landed by Soyuz.

2. Mark Shuttleworth

Mark Richard Shuttleworth (born 18 September 1973) is a South African-British entrepreneur who is the founder and CEO of Canonical, the company behind the development of the Linux-based Ubuntu operating system. In 2002, Shuttleworth became the first South African to travel to space as a space tourist, and indeed the first African from an independent country to travel to space. He is the second self-funded space tourist and the first South African in space. Flying through Space Adventures, he launched aboard the Russian Soyuz TM-34 mission as a spaceflight participant, paying approximately US$20,000,000.

3. Gregory Olsen

Gregory Hammond Olsen (born April 20, 1945) is an American entrepreneur, engineer, and scientist who, in October 2005, became the third private citizen to make a self-funded trip to the International Space Station with the company Space Adventures.Having flown to the International Space Station (ISS) with Soyuz TMA-7 (launched October 1, 2005, docked October 3) and landed with Soyuz TMA-6 (October 10), Olsen is the third self-funded space tourist to visit the ISS.Olsen has made some comments indicating that he is unhappy with the "space tourist" designation.

4. Anousheh Ansari

Anousheh Ansari, (born September 12, 1966, Mashhad, Iran), Iranian-born American businesswoman who was the first female space tourist, the first person of Iranian descent, and the first Muslim woman to go into space.Ansari has expressed that she does not consider herself a "space tourist," and prefers the title of "spaceflight participant." Ansari is a member of the X PRIZE Foundation's Vision Circle, as well as its Board of Trustees.Ansari trained as a backup for Daisuke Enomoto for a Soyuz flight to the International Space Station, through Space Adventures, Ltd. On August 21, 2006, Enomoto was medically disqualified from flying the Soyuz TMA-9 mission that was due to launch the following month. The next day Ansari was elevated to the prime crew.

SPACE TOURISM COMPANIES

1. Virgin Galactic

Virgin Galactic space tourism company is aiming to provide regular suborbital spaceflights for paying customers. Its current spaceplane, VSS Unity, entered outer space in December 2018 as part of its testing process, bringing the possibility of regular commercial spaceflights closer.

The company already has an extensive waiting list of people wishing to become space tourists, with an initial deposit of £200,000 required to secure a place on this list. However, Virgin Galactic has not been entire without issues, including multiple delays.

2.Blue Origin

To date, Blue Origin has been the main competitor for Virgin Galactic in terms of sub-orbital space travel tourism. However, their offering is based around a more traditional rocket, known as the New Shepard, which takes off and lands vertically, and their objectives are to build towards orbital spaceflight.

As with Virgin Galactic, the space tourism company has performed several test flights and is planning to put paying passengers into space soon. However, unlike Virgin Galactic, they have not started taking money for tickets. Their plans involve placing up to six passengers on each flight, with room to perform weightless somersaults.

3.SpaceX

SpaceX is already hugely experienced when it comes to launching space-bound flights and the company is also hoping to get on board the space tourism bandwagon. However, unlike most other companies operating in this field, they are prioritizing lunar tourism and other forms of space travel extending beyond Earth's orbit.

In 2017, the company's founder, Elon Musk, announced his intentions to send two paying customers on a trip around the moon on an inaugural lunar tourism mission. The mission was initially planned for 2018 but has since been delayed. SpaceX has not yet revealed any pricing strategy or waiting list for lunar trips.

INDIAN FOOTPRINT

In 1984, Indian Air Force pilot Rakesh Sharma made history by becoming the first Indian to travel to space. He is the retired Air Force Pilot who flew aboard Soyuz T-11 spacecraft under a joint Indian-Soviet programme and spent nearly eight days orbiting Earth. Notably, India-born late Kalpana Chawla and Indian-origin Sunita Williams flew into space as American astronauts.In the early 1960s, scientists launched a Nike-Apache rocket from TERLS, Kerala, igniting India's interest in space travel. In the 1970s, the Prime Minister of India established the Indian National Committee for Space Research, which later became the Indian Space Research Organisation (ISRO), which operated under a new independent Department of Space.

Santhosh George Kulangara (born 25 December 1971) is an Indian publisher, entrepreneur, and media person,travelled to more than 130 countries and his experiences and sights of journeys are telecasted through Sancharam, the first visual travelogue in Malayalam. He was the first Indian to be included among a group of people who paid to take a suborbital trip in a spaceship as part of the Virgin Galactic space tourism initiative and was labelled "India's first space tourist" by some outlets. He was selected for the trip in early 2007, and later that year he underwent a "zero gravity experience."

CHAPTER TWO

WANDERING ONE GATHERS HONEY

"The world is a book and those who do not travel read only one page."
~~Saint Augustine

DARK TOURISM

The philosophical investigation of death is the subject of dark tourism. Dark Tourism, also known as Thana tourism, black tourism, morbid tourism, grief tourism is a type of tourism that involves people taking a keen curiosity in visiting places that are historically linked to death and tragedy. Also, places that are reminders of human suffering and bloodshed are subsets of Dark Tourism. Dark places are more appealing because of their historical significance than their connotations with death and pain.

Visitors who are drawn to these areas go so with the objective of better understanding the Other's suffering or just for educational purposes. Dark Tourism imparts both a lesson to future generations as well as enhances the recipient capacity of society through the image of the Other.

CHARACTERISTICS OF DARK TOURISM

Dark tourism appears to have been a troublesome concept that began to get consideration as a tourism product in the early 1990s, but there is no evidence of its formulation or categorization. In reality, different terms were used to describe the same event:

"Black Spot" is a commercial improvement of grave and location sat which popular personalities or corpus people have faced with sudden and violent deaths.

"Thana tourism "-It is traveling to a place inspired with an aspiration to watch actual death or symbolic encounters with death.

"Atrocity Tourism"- It is a type of tourism that takes the individual to visit holocaust sites.

"Morbid Tourism"-It is the travel to places that emphasize accidents and sudden violent death.

Despite its irrationality, dark tourism is gaining popularity as a global travel trend that sends visitors to areas associated with sorrow, suffering, death, and devastation, as well as sites that are odd, risky, terrifying, and frequently bizarre. It leads us to places that are considered forbidden or taboo and can have strange consequences.

Dark Tourism sites exist to preserve and remember significant events, raise public awareness, and market the experience through domestic and international tourism. The public will be able to personally experience and comprehend the historic dark events through touching, feeling, and seeing them. It is, in fact, a sensible method of obtaining the lessons of the historical record

MOTIVES BEHIND A DARK TOURIST

- Eager to visit the place and feel the ingenuity, after knowing about the destination.
- Self-investigating and obtaining knowledge about such sites to brag about it in social groups
- Fascination, thrill, adventure, and excitement about the destination.
- Self- motives to prove self-maturity or adulthood.
- To pay their tribute, homage, or reflect on the disaster's outcome.
- Aspiration to search the truth through bizarre investigations
- The instinct to visit sites with famous memories linked with people or stories of haunted mansions etC.

DARK TOURISM IN INDIA

The concept of Dark tourism is slightly weird and hard to accept but apparently, it is a fast-catching latest trend in the world of India, which has a long history, hence Dark Tourism automatically finds its spot. India has experienced a lot of inglorious events in the past with its treasured gems with a long list of rulers, battles, and diversity which are often debated upon rather than celebrated. It enables the conveying of information about history including unsung heroes and their struggles. The tourists on traveling to actual sites experience a lot of struggles and tragedies that arouses interest in them and is a boon to those people who dislike reading history books and get curious about the past by actually visiting and confirming with their own eyes – seeing is believing! Dark tourism virtually gets the event in the past live like the tragic incidents that occurred and the historical image reflecting makes the region popular. India has a varied potential dark destination like the JallianwalaBagh Massacre in Amritsar, the Kuldhara village in Rajasthan, the haunted Savoy Hotel in Mussoorie or the 'Remember Bhopal' Museum in Madhya Pradesh.

IMPORTANT DARK TOURISM DESTINATION IN INDIA

1. JALLIANWALA BAGH, AMRITSAR (PUNJAB)

On 13 April 1919, a mass execution of mankind had taken place in the heart of Amritsar city. Thousands of innocent people were shot down to death who were protesting against British rule. The number of casualties recorded was approximately 1000 dead and around 1500 people were injured. Many of the people jumped in a well which is there in the premises to save their life from the continuous firing of bullets but that did not save their life. Many tourists visit this site to see the bullet holes and experience the helplessness of people at that moment under British rule.

2. CELLULAR JAIL, ANDAMAN & NICOBAR ISLAND (KALA PANI)

To torture and isolate the Indian freedom fighters, the British Indian government in 1906, made a Hell with concrete and iron rods. The Cellular Jail, in isolated Andaman & Nicobar Island which is popularly known as Kala Pani, Kala Pani then was also known as the prison of death. There were 80,000 prisoners in which hundreds of freedom fighters were sent to this jail for torturing them and isolating them from another world. The security of this jail was so high that no one has ever escaped from this jail except a great freedom fighter Vinayak Damodar Savarkar.

3. UNION CARBIDE FACTORY, BHOPAL (MADHYA PRADESH)

Bhopal gas tragedy was an industrial hazard that happened at Bhopal in Union Carbide subsidiary pesticide plant. 42 tons of Toxic Methyl Isocyanides (MIC) gas has been leaked due to the ignorance of maintenance of parts of the factory by high officials. which affected more than 500,000 people who were living around that area. The highly toxic substances in the air resulted in destroying the lungs of the people with a burning sensation in their lungs which led to thousands of immediate deaths. Now, this site is the most known and popular Dark Tourism destination in India.

4. KULDHARA VILLAGE, RAJASTHAN

Kuldhara Village, located around 20 kilometers from the Golden City Jaisalmeer is one of the most interesting and intriguing attractions. The village, which is rich with its fair share of legends and myths, is said to be a spooky and haunted village. The abandoned and eerily beautiful appearance of it, standing solitary amidst the vast stretches of desert, lives up to its reputation. There have been stories of ghostly and paranormal activities in and around the village, but like always no one could provide any solid proof of it.

5. TAJ PALACE HOTEL, MUMBAI

In November 2008, Mumbai city was attacked by 10 terrorists of the radical Islamic terrorist organization based in Pakistan. Killing 164 innocent people, the attack was a series of 12 coordinated shooting and bombing attacks that were continued for four days across Mumbai. Now, many tourists visit this site just to see and experience the helplessness of people under attack.

BACKPACKER TOURISM

Backpacker tourism is a type of youth travel that is mostly done by young people during gap years, although it can also be done by older individuals during a work break or retirement.

Backpacking is a low-cost, autonomous journey that frequently entails staying in cheap hotels and transporting all of one's belongings in a backpack. The backpacker packs all of his or her gear into a backpack. This gear must include food, water, and shelter, or the means to obtain them. A backpacking trip must include at least one overnight stay in the wilderness. Many backpacking trips last just a weekend but long-distance expeditions may last weeks or months.

A backpacker will always choose a low-cost accommodation, rather than staying in one place for an extended period of time, and will prefer for informal accommodation units given by the local community so that they can have intimate interactions with the hosts and learn about their culture. They travel with the sense of learning and gathering knowledge by gaining real experiences with the world, its people, nature. They are risk-averse individuals who travel solo and with a degree of freedom in their schedules. Backpackers differ from other sorts of travelers because of their independence and lack of tight plans.

CHARCHARACTERISTICS OF BACKPACKER

- Utilize public transportation, stay in low-cost accommodations such as hostels or homestays, and other methods of lowering costs.
- When compared to traditional vacations, this is a longer trip.

- Working in other countries for short stints, depending on work permit laws. It can also be undertaken by digital nomads, people who work using technology while living a nomadic lifestyle
- A quest for genuineness. Backpacking is seen as a form of education as well as a form of tourism. Backpackers prefer to visit a destination's "real" version rather than a packaged version associated with mass tourism.
- The desire to take part in or craft a narrative around traveling

CYBER TOURISM

Cyber tourism is a developing alternative type of tourism where information technologies, especially virtual reality technology, are widely used. Cyber tourism has led to a change in the traditional space conceptualization and has become increasingly emphasized in the context of tourism accessibility and smart tourism. Virtual reality is the technique which that supports Cyber tourism.

Virtual reality (VR) is a simulated experience that can be similar to or completely different from the real world. Applications of virtual reality include entertainment (particularly video games), education (such as medical or military training), and business (such as virtual meetings). Other distinct types of VR-style technology include augmented reality and mixed reality sometimes referred to as extended reality or XR. s virtual reality. Regardless of the type whether hotel or tourism destination, whether ski area, museum, or theme park, VR has the potential to create unforgettable experiences and memories for guests and customers.

When linking VR to tourism, some people might see VR as a tool to visit hotels, destinations, or attractions before physically traveling to a specific location. Although this is an option and might be useful in the planning process of a vacation, VR can also be much more than that.

For example, let's have a look at the American Museum of Natural History. One special exhibition introduces visitors to the time of dinosaurs, and to one of the most famous representatives of that time – the tyrannosaurus rex. While visitors can engage with interactive elements, fossils, and other familiar components of museums, the exhibition also offers a VR-multiplayer game. In this virtual world, visitors can work together as a team, use bones to build a skeleton of a tyrannosaurus rex, and bring the t-rex to life. Thus, letting players explore parts of nature, which they have never seen before

CHAPTER THREE

STORIES FROM THE COUNTRYSIDE

"Man cannot discover new oceans unless he has the courage to lose sight of the shore."
~~Andre Gide

RURAL TOURISM

UNWTO understands Rural Tourism as "a type of tourism activity in which the visitor's experience is related to a wide range of products generally linked to nature-based activities, agriculture, rural lifestyle/culture, angling, and sightseeing.

Rural Tourism activities take place in non-urban (rural) areas with the following characteristics:

2. low population density
3. landscape and land-use dominated by agriculture and forestry
4. traditional social structure and lifestyle".

Dimensions of Rural Tourism

Rural tourism showcases the rural life, art, culture, and heritage at rural locations, thereby benefiting the local community economically and socially as well as enabling interaction between the tourists and the locals for a more enriching tourism experience.

1. Agritourism

Although often used to describe all tourism activities in rural areas, more frequently either term relates to tourism products which are 'directly connected with the agrarian environment, agrarian products or agrarian stays': staying at the farm, whether in rooms or camping, educational visits, meals, recreational activities, and the sale of a farm product or handicrafts.

2. Farm Tourism

Perfectly farm-related and most usually associated with tourism involving staying in farm accommodation and seeking experiences from farm operations and attractions.

3. Wilderness and Forest Tourism

Tourists explore the wilderness and natural beauty of the rural area. It may be implicitly included within notions of rural tourism, or they may be regarded as separate. In wilderness and forest tourism, tourists travel to the natural habitat of plants and animals. It mostly encompasses non-consumptive interactions with wildlife and nature, such as observing and photographing animals in their natural habitats.

4. Green Tourism

Green tourism refers to tourism in the countryside or green areas. It is more commonly used to describe forms of tourism that are considered to be more environmentally friendly than traditional, mass tourism. In rural areas, green tourism is an important form of rural tourism. Green tourism is portrayed as an approach to tourism development that seeks to develop a symbiotic relationship with the physical and social environment on which it depends and implicitly seeks to attain sustainability ideals.

5.Ecotourism

it is a form of nature tourism (tourism to natural, unspoiled areas) that assumes active promotion of environmental conservation and direct benefits for local societies and cultures, together with the provision for tourists of a positive, educative experience. Ecotourism is a group of sustainable tourism activities occurred in the natural environment.

BRANDING RURAL TOURISM

- Untapped tourism potential like medical, rural, tribal, eco, adventure, heritage, spiritual, food, and many more are being explored in recent times.
- Thus, the witness of practicing tourism nowadays has been shifted from traditional to non-traditional thrusts.
- Many key concepts like sustainable tourism development, alternate tourism, pro-poor tourism, volunteer tourism, responsible tourism, green tourism, community-based tourism, special interest tourism, etc. are being coined.
- The developments of Rural Tourism have now gained popularity and proved to be a sword with double edge i.e., source of employment for the local community (Pro-poor Tourism) and preserving its rich culture and heritage (Sustainable Development).

Benefits of Rural Tourism

- Employment generation – The major advantage of promoting rural tourism is the creation of employment opportunities, especially for those who do not have agricultural land to meet their economic needs. As tourism requires a multitude of services, local community members can engage themselves in a variety of economic activities like accommodation, food, and beverages, local guides, artisans, etc.
- Preservation of local tradition – As tourists visit rural areas to feel authentic rural settings, tourism provides economic incentives to preserve cultures and traditions. With increased urbanization and

globalization, people are adopting global products leaving behind the local tradition. Rural tourism encourages local communities to revive and preserve their traditions, crafts, traditional festivals, architecture, and other unique practices.

- Developing new skills – The entire tourism and hospitality industry requires specific skills to cater to the tourist. The local community members start learning new skill sets once the tourist begins visiting the local areas.
- Cultural exchange – It also promotes culture as a local community shares their culture and traditions with the tourists and in the process also learns about their cultures.
- Reduces Urban drift – One of the challenges countries are facing is the movement of rural people to urban areas. With the promotion of rural tourism, urban drift reduces as people get employment opportunities in their region. Further with the emergence of tourism, infrastructural development also takes place it encourages people to stay in their areas rather than migrating to the urban centers.
- Improves Quality of life – As social interaction takes place between tourists and local people; rural tourism has an enormous potential to enhance the Quality of life of the residents. As they have access to global information, products, and services. Further, the local government also starts building up infrastructure like roads, electricity, hospitals, etc. as they see the movement of tourists in this region.
- Entrepreneurship opportunities – The tourism industry has an enormous potential to create new business opportunities, as interested people can venture to a variety of support services. There are immense entrepreneurial opportunities that can be generated on account of the rural tourism business.
- Builds Community pride – Rural tourism can also promote community diversification as local people can start leveraging their existing resources for economic and social benefit. Communities that have unique resources can earn their livelihood by strengthening their skills, thereby enhancing community pride.
- Environmental Benefits – with the increased tourist movement in any community, there is a risk of ecological degradation. But to preserve authenticity, landscape conservation can be promoted. It can also encourage local communities to adopt environmentally friendly

practices.

- Sustainable livelihood – Rural tourism has the potential to provide sustainable livelihood to rural communities as a source of income irrespective of the seasonality factor. As rural economies are predominantly agriculture-based, there is always a risk of seasonality which can affect the income-generating opportunities for rural people. In such a scenario the rural tourism can be a sustainable livelihood mechanism for rural people.
- Women empowerment – As tourism increases in rural communities, there are higher chances for women to be a part of the growing village economy. Women workforce can be engaged in various tourism service delivery processes like housekeeping, food and beverages, and others.

RURAL TOURISM IN INDIA

India has the fourth most considerable number of world heritage sites in the world, from Kashmir to Kanyakumari there are so many beautiful places in the country that anyone would say heaven, and the beauty that lies in any rural India is incomparable.

Ministry of Tourism in India has laid a great deal of emphasis on the development of such rural tourism sites which boast rich art, culture, handloom, heritage, and crafts. These villages are affluent in both natural beauty and cultural splendour.

India bears the massive potential of tourism in rural India. 70% of the population lives in rural India dependent solely on agriculture or small and cottage industry. And there is a need for the creation of newer opportunities and that can be fulfilled through rural tourism.

Ministry of Tourism GOI, under its rural tourism schemes, has identified around 153 rural locations across the country. Thirty-six rural sites are also supported by the United Nations development program for capacity building.

The government of India is providing a fund to the local destinations for the development of possible kinds of rural activities. While developing the policy, the government has emphasized building up both hardware (tourism infrastructure) and software (capacity building).

Each village will be categorized based on its unique resource. Then the appropriate strategy will be equipped to promote the town. In the last few decades, a trend of increased urbanization has been witnessed across the world and even in India, causing stress and limited economic opportunities. The government of Indian has an independent Ministry that looks into Rural Development which aims to social transformation of rural societies through economic empowerment. Tourism has been identified as a potent tool to transform agrarian societies by involving communities in the developmental process.

VOLUNTARY TOURISM

volunteer tourism is a type of tourism where an individual will travel abroad to a destination that is predominantly considered 'undeveloped' or 'developing' to offer their support to those in need. And when we use the phrase 'those in need', which is expressed a lot in volunteering, we refer to those who are surrounded by extreme poverty, do not have adequate education and healthcare facilities, and frequently have little building infrastructure. Volunteer tourism is a specific form of tourism, designed purposely to provide a product or service to meet the needs of a particular market segment, meaning it falls under the umbrella of niche tourism. work they do can be related to agriculture, health care, education, and many other areas.

BENEFITS OF VOLUNTARY TOURISM

- If the voluntourism opportunity is well-thought-out and sustainable, a volunteer's actions can have a long-term impact.
- The opportunity to immerse in a community, to surround yourself with new friends and activities, and to see the issues a community faces, broadens your scope of the world and your understanding of the complex nature of poverty and sustainable development.
- Travel stimulates local economies, and voluntarists can do just that when they purchase goods from local markets, go on tours and excursions on their days off, and eat at local restaurants. This is great for businesses operating in the community and country.

- Rather than providing inferior quality work, voluntourism can have a large impact if the work an individual is doing matches their skillset.

CRITICISMS OF VOLUNTEER TOURISM

- Local resources are drained: Communities receiving volunteers want to be great hosts, so they pour their resources into ensuring food and accommodations are sufficient. These resources could be better used to improve their own lives. While volunteers may consider themselves a helpful source of manpower doing good work, they are just another mouth to feed.
- Volunteers are inexperienced: One of the biggest arguments against voluntourism is the lack of related experience volunteers have for the work they're expected to do in the field.
- Not enough time: Volunteer vacations usually only last between a few days to a couple of weeks. Since most of that time is spent working, volunteers miss out on opportunities to gain a deeper understanding of the culture of the country they're visiting.
- Local economy is disrupted: When volunteers show up to do work, they're often putting local laborers out of work. In the case of the housing volunteer, local masons, construction workers, and carpenters lose jobs because of inexperienced foreign laborers.
- Poor supervision: Local communities are more prone to exploitation when voluntourists have inadequate supervision. Voluntarists may not mean any harm, but working with vulnerable people requires a stricter set of standards

SOCIAL TOURISM

Social tourism is making tourism available to poor people who otherwise could not afford to travel for their education or recreation. It includes youth hostels and low-priced holiday accommodation run by church and voluntary organizations, trade unions, or in Communist times publicly owned enterprises. In May 1959, at the second Congress of Social Tourism in Austria, Walter Hunziker proposed the following definition:

"Social tourism is a type of tourism practiced by low-income groups, and which is rendered possible and facilitated by entirely separate and therefore easily recognizable services"

social tourism activity had emerged across Europe from the nineteenth century, alongside the development of transport (particularly rail) infrastructure, economic advances, and social reforms, specifically in connection with the development of the labour movement, and was complemented through related activities by worker's collectives, non-profit associations, cooperatives and trades unions. The 'rational recreation' movement, improved that productive and upright leisure and recreation would benefit society and crucially, create a more productive workforce.

social tourism not only from the perspective of care for the disadvantaged travellers but also as their potential employer. Social tourism will attract lower-income groups and those who are physically and mentally retarded. Studies observed increased awareness in attracting those travellers falling under the social tourist category, in off-seasons. Business units and institutions with solely profit interest simply cannot be defending and representing the interest of social tourist welfare, which by definition falls into the category of "financially low performing accounts" and this way falling out of category "source or the feeding market". Consequently, it is possible to conclude, that it can only be the government and non-governmental or not-for-profit organizations, which genuinely care for disadvantaged social tourists, with no profit drive in their mind.

However, the social organisation of travel for leisure predates the mass factory production era. Indeed, Thomas Cook's first tours were established through the idea that travel could be morally and spiritually enlightening and thus provided a positive use of leisure time. The origins of social tourism lay in the idea that tourism provides positive and important recuperative and educational benefits for ordinary people, and that such opportunities should be extended to all people in society.

CHAPTER FOUR

STAY IN YOUR LANE

"THE REAL VOYAGE OF DISCOVERY CONSISTS NOT IN SEEKING NEW LANDSCAPES, BUT IN HAVING NEW EYES."
~~MARCEL PROUST

SEX TOURISM

Sex tourism is the movement of people from their usual place of residence to another location for a minimum period of twenty-four hours to a maximum of six months for the sole purpose of having sex and sexual activities. Sex tourism has meant that individuals buy sex from sex workers; however, modern sex tourism is a more complicated matter than this. This is perhaps the most controversial and condemned aspect of tourism

According to United Nations, World Tourism Organization (UNWTO) sex tourism is defined as, "trips organized from within the sector, or from outside the tourism sector but using its structures and networks with the primary purpose of effecting a commercial sexual relationship by the tourist with the residents at the destination."

Sex tourism is usually associated with prostitution, Prostitution is the exchange of sexual services for money. Prostitution is perhaps the most well-known form of sex tourism and has been around since before records began Sometimes prostitution will be very blatant. For example, Spain is famous for having prostitutes lining the streets looking for business and, in the Philippines, where 'happy ending massages' are a popular choice amongst travellers. Although the sex tourism industry also encompasses the search for 'mail brides', sex shows, and sex slavery. Popular sex tourism destinations include Amsterdam, Thailand, and The

Gambia. Tourists involved with sex activities are not always categorised as sex tourists. This is perhaps due to the ambiguities in the definition and the common perceptual parameters limiting a sex tourist to one who directly pays for sex.

Sex work is a predominant reason for world travel and is extremely profitable. The market can become exceedingly exploitive and unethically abused as tourists are motivated to engage in sexual conduct due to the untraceable nature and lack of law enforcement control, especially with accessibility to minors. Men who seek women as sexual partners are the most common demographic involved in sex tourism. Other demographics include; female sex tourism (women seeking men), men seeking men, and adults seeking children.

Over recent years, adult-only sex resorts have become the popular alternative for travellers wanting to experience consensual sex abroad whilst avoiding the ethical issues of paid sexual activity. Those resorts are characterized as safe, consensual spaces, and sexually positive nature, where all expressions of gender, orientation, and relationships are free of any pressure.

INDIAN SCENARIO

India is one of the fastest-growing developing countries today, still, there are some dark corners in this country, that are lagging, at present. In India, the abuse of both male and female children by tourists has acquired serious dimensions.

In India, prostitution is legal. Selling sex, kerb crawling, owning or managing a brothel, prostitution in a hotel, child prostitution, pimping, and pandering are all prohibited activities. Many brothels, however, are operating illegally in Indian cities such as Mumbai, Delhi, Bangalore, Kolkata, and Chennai.

Goa and Kerala were the places often visited by tourists in search of child sex and beach boys, shack owners, and former victims of pedophiles were facilitating the procurement of boys and girls for sex. It is hard to believe, that in the present scenario, India habituates some places where girls of the families are forced into prostitution, even before they reach puberty.

Sonagachi is the largest red-light district in Asia with several hundred multi-story brothels and an estimated 16,000 sex workers (2020) contained within the area. Sonagachi is a red-light neighbourhood in Kolkata, India, located in North Kolkata near the intersection of Jatindra Mohan Avenue.

CHILD SEX TOURISM

Some tourists that engage with sex tourism, will specifically travel to engage in sex with children. While it is criminal in most countries, this industry is believed to involve as many as 2 million children around the world. Thailand is considered to have the worst child sex trafficking record, followed closely by Brazil. Users of children for commercial and sexual purposes can be categorized by motive. Two types of abuser's preferential abusers prefer children because they want to build a relationship with them or because they believe the risk of sexually transmitted infections is lower with them; and situational abusers who do not actively seek out children but act based on circumstance. To eradicate the practice, some countries have enacted laws that allow the prosecution of their citizens for child abuse that occurs outside their home country, even if it is not against the law in the country where the child abuse took place.

Child prostitution usually manifests in the form of sex trafficking, in which a child is kidnapped or tricked into becoming involved in the sex trade, or survival sex, in which the child engages in sexual activities to procure essentials such as food and shelter. Prostitution of children is commonly associated with child pornography, and they often overlap. Some people travel to foreign countries to engage in child sex tourism.

According to experts, modern technology and cheap travel have further perpetuated the problem of child sex tourism. Technology has also proved to be a safe space to carry out such activities and share child pornography without being caught due to the anonymity it offers. Child sexual predators have found a way to reach young children through the internet and messaging applications which gives rise to romance tourism. Romance tourism is when the tourists meet the children online and strike a conversation with them and make the children comfortable without hinting at any sexual intention.

According to a report by the National Human Rights Commission (NHRC), India is fast becoming a hotspot for child sex tourism, with children being exploited in the name of pilgrimage, heritage, and coastal tourism. Maharashtra, Goa, Karnataka, Kerala, Tamil Nadu, Andhra Pradesh, West Bengal, and Orissa are some of the common hotspots for this immoral and illegal trade. Factors leading to the growth of child sex tourism in India are Poverty, Consumerism and Materialism, Dysfunctional family background, Migration or unemployment, Illiteracy or out-of-school children, Procurement within families, etc.

TERRORISM AND POLITICAL CRISES EFFECTS ON TOURISM

Tourists are often regarded as longing for relaxing and unconcerned holiday making and therefore are sensitive to events of violence in holiday destinations. Ironically, or most of human history, traveling has been associated with risk and integrity and the belonging of the traveller.

The US Department of State defines terrorism as "premeditated, politically motivated violence perpetrated against civilians and unarmed military personnel by subnational groups usually intended to influence an audience"; and international terrorism as "involving citizens or the territory of more than one country".

Political instability describes the condition of a country where a government "has been toppled, or is controlled by factions following a coup, or where basic functional pre-requisites for social-order control and maintenance are unstable and periodically disrupted". Terrorism and political instability are not unrelated, aside from terrorism, international, regional, and civil wars, ethnic cleansing, declarations of martial law, military coups, and riots can often be traced to political unrest, threatening both the safety of specific countries and of entire regions.

On 26 June 2015, 38 people, mostly British tourists, were killed by a gunman at a tourist resort in Port El Kantaoui, just outside the city of Sousse in Tunisia. Not to mention the human tragedy, the immediate economic consequences were devastating for an economy that gets almost 15% of its GDP from tourism: several tour operators and air carriers adjusted or even canceled tourist bookings in the months that followed the attack.

Terrorism and crime have been acknowledged as negative factors entailing both direct costs (value of damaged structures, lives lost or damaged, injuries sustained, etc.) and indirect costs (higher insurance premiums, higher security costs, and lost commerce).Tourists want to travel to safe places if they see a risk of injury or death, or even just becoming involved in a stressful situation, they will avoid that destination. When violence becomes widespread and prolonged, governments in tourists' origin countries will advise against travelling to the destination.

Political instability and Terrorism that targets tourism as a disaster for a destination and ensuing events can create a serious tourism crisis. Tourist destinations especially those vulnerable to politically motivated violence should incorporate crisis management planning into their overall sustainable development and marketing or management strategies to protect and rebuild their image of safety or attractiveness, to reassure potential visitors of the safety of the area, to re-establish the area's functionality or attractiveness, and to aid local travel and tourism industry members in their economic recovery. Recommendations include having a crisis management plan in place, establishing a tourism crisis management task force, developing a crisis management guidebook, and partnering with law enforcement officials.

CLIMATE CHANGE AND TOURISM

Tourism can play a significant role in addressing climate change if the innovativeness and resources of this vital global economic sector are fully mobilized and oriented towards this goal. The concern of the tourism community regarding the challenge of climate change has visibly increased over the last five years. The World Tourism Organization (UNWTO) and several partner organizations, including UNEP, convened the First International Conference on Climate Change and Tourism in Djerba, Tunisia in 2003.

Impacts of Climate Change

According to the World Tourism Organization, impacts from climate change on tourism include the following (2008)

1. Direct climate impacts

They are changes that occur as a result of warming trends, cooling trends, or extreme weather events. Examples include a lack of snow to operate mountain resorts, melting glaciers in mountainous regions, and floods, landslides, and wildfires that could affect tourist areas.

2. Indirect environmental change impacts

They are the by-products of climate change. Global temperature changes may create water shortages, a loss of biodiversity, impacts on landscape aesthetics, and damage to infrastructure through extreme weather events. Examples in tourism include the inability to maintain resort facilities in desert environments due to water shortages, erosion of tropical atolls from rising sea levels, extinction of valuable wildlife species due to changes in habitat, and increased costs of maintaining infrastructure in the face of environmental change.

Major climate change impacts and implications for tourism destinations

- Warmer temperatures: Altered seasonality, heat stress for tourists, cooling costs, changes in plant-wildlife-insect populations and distribution, infectious disease ranges.
- Decreasing snow cover and shrinking glaciers: Lack of snow in winter destinations increased snow-making costs, shorter winter sports seasons aesthetics of landscape reduced Increasing frequency and intensity of extreme storms.
- Reduced precipitation and increased evaporation: In some regions, Water shortages, competition over water between tourism and other sectors, competition for water between visitors and residents, desertification, increased wildfires threatening infrastructure, and affecting demand
- Sea level rise: Coastal erosion, loss of beach area, higher costs to protect and maintain waterfronts. Sea surface temperatures rise Increased coral bleaching and marine resource and aesthetics degradation in dive and snorkel destinations increased invasive

species in waterways

- Changes in terrestrial and marine biodiversity: Loss of natural attractions and species from destinations, higher risk of diseases in tropical-subtropical countries (e.g., heavy rainfall leading to an increase in dengue fever and malaria)
- Forest fires Loss of natural attractions: An increase of flooding risk; damage to tourism infrastructure
- Soil changes (e.g., moisture levels, erosion, and acidity) Loss of archaeological assets and other natural resources, with impacts on destination attractions

CHAPTER FIVE

UNION WITH DIVINE

"All journeys have secret destinations of which the traveller is unaware."
~~ Martin Buber

HEALTH TOURISM

Health tourism covers those types of tourism which have as a primary motivation, the contribution to physical, mental, and/or spiritual health through medical and wellness-based activities which increase the capacity of individuals to satisfy their own needs and function better as individuals in their environment and society.

Health tourism is the umbrella term for the subtypes: wellness tourism and medical tourism.

Medical tourism is a type of tourism activity that involves the use of evidence-based medical healing resources and services (both invasive and non-invasive). This may include diagnosis, treatment, cure, prevention, and rehabilitation.

Wellness tourism is a type of tourism activity that aims to improve and balance all of the main domains of human life including physical, mental, emotional, occupational, intellectual, and spiritual. The primary motivation for wellness tourism is to engage in preventive, proactive, lifestyle-enhancing activities such as fitness, healthy eating, relaxation, pampering, and healing treatments.

Earlier, health tourism was used to describe people who travelled from less-developed countries to prominent health centres in developed countries for treatment that was not available at home. In current history, however, it has also come to apply to people from wealthy nations who travel to developing countries for cheaper medical treatment. Medical services that are unavailable or unlicensed in the homeland may also be a motivator. Medical tourism most often is for surgeries (cosmetic or otherwise) or similar treatments, though people also travel for dental tourism or fertility tourism. People with rare conditions may travel to countries where the treatment is better understood. However, almost all types of health care are available, including psychiatry, alternative medicine, convalescent care, and even burial services.

The first recorded instance of people travelling for medical treatment dates back thousands of years to when Greek pilgrims travelled from the eastern Mediterranean to a small area in the Saronic Gulf called Epidauria. The high expense of health care, long wait periods for certain treatments, the convenience and affordability of international travel, and improvements in both technology and standards of care in many nations are all factors that have contributed to the growing popularity of medical tourism. Popular medical travel worldwide destinations include Canada, Cuba, Costa Rica, Ecuador, India, Israel, Jordan, Malaysia, Mexico, Singapore, South Korea, Taiwan, Thailand, Turkey, United States. However, perceptions of medical tourism are not always positive. In places like the US, which has high standards of quality, medical tourism is viewed as risky. In some parts of the world, wider political issues can influence where medical tourists will choose to seek out health care. The quality of post-operative care can also vary dramatically, depending on the hospital and country. moreover, health facilities that treat medical tourists may lack an acceptable grievances policy to handle complaints from disappointed patients promptly and ethically.

The World Health Organization recognised differences in healthcare provider standards around the world and established the World Alliance for Patient Safety in 2004. This organisation aids hospitals and governments all over the world in developing patient safety policies and practices, which are especially important while offering medical tourism services. Nurse case managers are often provided by companies that specialize in medical value travel to assist patients with pre-and post-travel medical difficulties. They may also be able to assist in the provision of resources for follow-up care when the patient returns.

MEDICAL TOURISM IN INDIA

At a time when global healthcare costs are sky-rocketing, the world can take a leaf or two from the Indian healthcare sector, which provides high-quality healthcare facilities at a highly competitive price compared to other similar healthcare facilities in the world. This makes India a great destination for healthcare both for modern as well as traditional medicine and therapy

Medical tourism is a growing sector in India. In 2017, 495,056 patients visited India to seek medical care. Most of the medical tourist arrivals were from Southeast Asia, the Middle East, Africa, and the SAARC region. The city of Chennai has come to be known as the healthcare capital of India.

India is a leading player in the medical tourist/healthcare industry. It is increasingly emerging as the destination of choice for a wide range of medical procedures. There are numerous advantages of going to India for treatment. Some of the advantages of going to India for medical treatment are:

- Internationally accredited medical facilities using the latest technologies.
- Highly qualified Physicians/Surgeons and hospital support staff.
- Significant cost savings compared to domestic private healthcare. Medical treatment costs in India are lower by at least 60-80% when compared to similar procedures in North America and the UK.
- No Wait Lists
- Fluent English-speaking staff
- Options for a private room, translator, private chef, dedicated staff during the stay, and many other tailor-made services.
- Can easily be combined with a holiday/business trip

India is renowned for ancient alternative therapies such as Ayurveda, Yoga and Meditation, and Therapeutic Massage. India is an exotic tourist destination offering everything from beaches, mountains, cosmopolitan cities, quaint villages, and pilgrimages to suit every palate. Rich in history and culture, India has proved to be an oasis in the modern world, providing complete health and wellbeing, while providing the latest in technology.

The Indian healthcare industry also competes with the best in the world in terms of, infrastructure, technology, specialist doctors, and nurses. The country has the finest and one of the largest pools of doctors and paramedics in South Asia, with many of them being of global repute. India's expertise in highly specialized areas of organ transplants, cardiology, oncology, etc. has made India an emerging hotspot for medical value travel.

The healthcare industry of India is expanding at an extraordinary rate. Government investment, private hospitals, and foreign aid in public health programs play key roles in this boom. The Government has recently taken concrete steps to make India stand out in the area of medical value travel. The government's vision and intention, to promote and develop India can be gauged by the fact that four ministries (Ministry of Health and Family Welfare, Ministry of Tourism, Ministry of Commerce, and Ministry of AYUSH), along with SEPC and NABH, are involved in promoting India, globally, as the preferred destination for medical tourism. The government has also set up a 'National Medical & Wellness Tourism Promotion Board' to look into the various issues such as Regulatory; Accreditation and Marketing to give the highest assurance to travellers.

SUPER SPECIALITY TREATMENTS FOR TOURIST

CARDIAC SURGERY

Cardiac surgery, also known as cardiovascular surgery, is a type of surgery performed by cardiac surgeons on the heart or blood vessels. Heart transplantation is also part of it. India has an association with the best cardiac surgeons and hospitals, providing world-class treatment at affordable rates.

- Qualified panel: India has a network of the best surgeons and hospitals, providing supreme healthcare.
- Affordable: The expenses incurred in the entire travel for cardiac surgery in India are nearly 30% of that in most Western countries.
- Professionalism: Indian doctors and other health professionals maintain the highest ethics in providing the treatments and the

procedures are followed with transparency.

- Other services: Indian hospitals also takes care of facilities like providing health meals as prescribed by your doctor, planning a vacation in India, rejuvenation, rehab facilities, etc.

The best cardiac surgeons in India provide specialist consulting, diagnostic, and treatment services at different locations in India. The major cardiac hospitals in India are located at Chennai, Delhi, Pune, Kochi, Jaipur, Chandigarh, Mumbai, Bangalore, Ahmedabad, Gurgaon, Noida, Nagpur, Kerala, Goa, Hyderabad, etc.

ORGAN TRANSPLANTATION

Organ transplantation is a medical procedure in which an organ is removed from one body and placed in the body of a recipient, to replace a damaged or missing organ. The donor and recipient may be at the same location, or organs may be transported from a donor site to another location.

Organ transplantation is a life-saving therapy for end-stage organ failure. The most commonly transplanted organs are the kidney, liver, heart, lungs, pancreas, and intestines.

There are two types of organ donation:

i. Living Donor Organ Donation: A person during his life can donate one kidney (the other kidney is capable of maintaining the body functions adequately for the donor), a portion of the pancreas (half of the pancreas is adequate for sustaining pancreatic functions) and a part of the liver (the segments of the liver will regenerate after a period of time in both recipient and donor). A living Donor is any person not less than 18 years of age, who voluntarily authorizes the removal of any of his organ and/or tissue, during his or her lifetime, as per prevalent medical practices for therapeutic purposes.

ii. Deceased Donor Organ Donation: A person can donate multiple organs and tissues after (brain-stem/cardiac) death. His/her organ continues to live in another person's body. A deceased Donor is anyone, regardless of age, race or gender can become an organ and tissue donor after his or her Death (Brainstem/ Cardiac). Consent of a near relative or a person in lawful possession of the dead body is required.

The Transplantation of Human Organs and Tissues Act, 1994 governs organ donation in India. Organ donation is legal for both deceased and living donors. It also recognises death as a form of brain death. The National Organ and Tissue Transplant Organisation (NOTTO) is the governing body for all organ procurement, allotment, and distribution activities in the country.

TRANSPLANT TOURISM

According to WHO, "transplant tourism" refers to patients travelling across the borders to be transplanted elsewhere. People tend to travel for transplantation, either because it is not available in their home countries, such as Tajikistan and Azerbaijan, or if the facilities are adequate in their homeland, there are not enough organs available.

"Transplant tourists" are traveling to established destinations to obtain readily accessible organs for transplantation. Transplant tourism is fuelled by the demand of desperate patients who are willing to pay large sums of money to obtain a kidney or, less frequently, a liver lobe from a living donor. It is also fuelled by the willingness of some physicians to take part in this criminal activity, in order to profit from it. Transplant tourism typically involves the movement of recipients to countries where the vulnerable and impoverished serve as an organ source and where surgical procedures are undertaken. However, recently other forms of transplant tourism have emerged.

The Health Ministry has made it mandatory for foreign nationals seeking organ transplants in India to be registered in the waiting list of hospitals following reports claiming they were being given preferential treatment by some private institutions. Also, an organ can be allotted to a foreign national only if there is no Indian recipient available to receive the donated organ at that time of allocation. Among the patients from abroad, NRIs and persons of Indian origin will be given preference.

KEYHOLE SURGERY

Laparoscopy is a type of surgical procedure that allows a surgeon to access the inside of the abdomen (tummy) and pelvis without having to make large incisions in the skin. This procedure is also known as keyhole surgery or minimally invasive surgery. Large incisions can be avoided during laparoscopy because the surgeon uses an instrument called a laparoscope. This is a small tube that has a light source and a camera, which relays images of the inside of the abdomen or pelvis to a television monitor.

The advantages of this technique over traditional open surgery include:

- a shorter hospital stays and faster recovery time
- less pain and bleeding after the operation
- reduced scarring

The cost of Laparoscopic surgery in India is significantly cheaper when compared to the US, UK, Singapore, etc. When these factors are taken into consideration, the cost of one Laparoscopic Surgery in India on an average is USD 500 to USD 1100, whereas, the same surgery in the US costs around USD 5,000 to USD 10,000.

COSMETIC SURGERY

Cosmetic surgery is a type of plastic surgery that aims to improve a person's appearance. Plastic surgery is a surgical specialty that focuses on restoring, reconstructing, or changing the human body. Reconstructive surgery and cosmetic surgery are the two main types of surgery. Craniofacial surgery, hand surgery, microsurgery, and burn treatment are all examples of reconstructive surgery. While reconstructive surgery aims to rebuild or improve the function of a body part, cosmetic (or aesthetic) surgery aims to improve its appearance.

India has rapidly become a hot favourite Plastic & cosmetic surgery destination for medical tourists from worldwide because people get world-class facilities at more affordable and economical costs, higher success rates, and safety measures. Indian plastic surgeons already have a great reputation when it comes to the finest surgical skills for providing a wide range of cosmetic as well as plastic surgery procedures. With the increasing popularity and easy availability of such procedures in India, more and more foreigners are flying in to get chiselled looks while experiencing the vast heritage of this ancient country. It sounds amazing to spend the recovery period visiting historic places, indulging in cultural activities and authentic food.

CHAPTER SIX

THE BUSINESS AND PLEASURE OF TEETH AND REPRODUCTION

"Leave The Road; Take The Trials "
~~Pythagore

DENTAL TOURISM

Dentistry, also known as dental medicine or oral medicine, is a branch of medicine that studies, diagnoses, prevents, and treats diseases, disorders, and conditions of the oral cavity (mouth), particularly the dentition (development and arrangement of teeth) and oral mucosa, as well as adjacent and related structures and tissues, particularly associated with Jaw and facial area.

Dental tourism is a subset of the sector known as medical tourism. Also found under the heading of Dental Vacations. It involves individuals seeking dental care outside of their local healthcare systems usually in combination with taking a vacation to a foreign country.

Dental Tourism is a budding concept for a planned vacation along with total Dental solutions and care. Dental treatment is very costly in most of European and American countries. By opting for dental tourism, one can enjoy holidays and receive services related to Dentistry such as Dental Implants at a very affordable price.

The main reason for going abroad for medical tourism is access to world-class dental care. Furthermore, the favourable price level makes dental care of the highest international standards available to everyone.

However, price should not be considered the main factor in deciding to have surgery abroad.

India is emerging as one of the preferred destinations for dental tourism in the world. Thousands of people from USA, Europe, and other parts of the world fly to India every year seeking dental treatment. Though tourists attach a variety of reasons for their travel, the major indicator is the cost for dental implants and dental surgery, which is generally cheap in India.

The idea of traveling outside of your country to obtain dental care, or dental tourism, is rapidly becoming a very attractive option for those people who need cosmetic dentistry procedures, restorative dental care, and routine dental treatment. US and UK citizens have been attracted to India for their dental work that is affordable of high quality. India has highly trained dental care professionals and very good dental clinics. There are many international flights to India so traveling would be not a problem. There are people from all around the world who have started considering India as one of the best places in the world to receive affordable dental care.

Cities are known for being the Best Place for Dental Tourism in India;

Mumbai Hyderabad Kerala
   Delhi Pune Goa
   Bangalore Nagpur Jaipur
   Chennai Gurgaon Chandigarh

Dental Treatments/Procedures Offered by Dental Tourism in India:

India is well equipped with quality hospitals and experienced dentists that assure reliable treatment. Many dental tourism providers in India offer worthwhile dental packages. Most of them include the following dental surgery/treatment options:

- Intra mouth dental scanning
- Extraction of normal/fractured teeth under local anesthesia
- Extraction of impacted wisdom teeth

- Maxillary Surgery
- Dental Bridges, Porcelain/Ceramic crowns
- Bleaching
- Prosthesis on the implant/ Dental Implants
- Vertical and horizontal bone grafting
- Gum Grafting/ Gums treatment
- Palatal orthodontics
- Fluoride treatments for children
- Cosmetic dentistry
- Smile designing
- Root Canal
- Teeth whitening
- Tooth contouring and reshaping
- Dental Fillings

BENIFITS OF HAVING DENTAL TREATMENT IN INDIA

1. Low Cost

Dental tourism is a great money saver. That is the biggest attraction for most to go abroad for dental treatment. The economy of all developing countries is such that all amenities like food and shelter and education and treatment charges are low.

2. High Quality

The fact that it is cheap does not make these dental services inferiors. The doctors are well trained and often many of them have studied and trained in western countries. Apart from this, they also possess modern equipment and state-of-the-art technology.

3. Immediate Service

Avoidance in time delay is another attraction. Most agencies understand the importance of the problem and they are very quick in their service.

4. Great Convenience

Comprehensive packages by agencies make sure that they take care of all aspects of an overseas dental appointment. Their comprehensive package ensures that the patient gets the necessary information and contacts immediately.

5. Travel Opportunities

As the name dental tourism implies, those traveling abroad for dental care are combining the pleasures of a vacation with dental treatment. In most of the developing countries that dental appointments are made, boarding and lodging, and traveling also come cheap. So, it would be most ideal to combine dental treatment with a pleasure trip. Most dental care seekers turn medical care into a holiday by opting to get appointments on weekends and taking along family or friends with them.

FERTILITY TOURISM

Fertility tourism (also known as reproductive tourism or cross-border reproductive care) is the practice of seeking fertility treatment in another country or jurisdiction. It is a type of medical tourism. When a woman is unable to have a clinical pregnancy after 12 months of intercourse attempts, she is considered to have fertility issues. Infertility, or the inability to conceive, affects 8-12 percent of couples who want to start a family.

The main procedures sought are in vitro fertilization (IVF), artificial insemination by a donor, as well as surrogacy. These methods are types of assisted reproductive technology. Each of these three methods have varying popularity in different countries, with one method being more sought after in these destinations compared to another method in another country.

People are drawn to fertility tourism for a variety of reasons, including a lack of resources and high costs, as well as cultural, religious, legal, and safety and efficacy concerns. Others who are infertile, single, older, or identify as a member of the LGBTQIA+ community have an impact on the need for fertility treatments from other countries. As a result of these worsening conditions, people are being forced to travel to other countries in order to receive fertility treatments that are not available in their own countries.

Although not strictly tourism, the fertility centres around the country promote their services as "IVF holidays" or "A Holiday with a Purpose", offering clients a relaxing and calming environment while undergoing fertility treatment.Despite the commonality of vacation-like experience, reproductive tourism differs from medical tourism in as much as it relies on third parties to contribute their gametes or gestate or give birth for patients to make use of ARTs. Globalisation combined with international trade agreements, advances in ARTs, electronic communication, and low-cost travel have made reproductive tourism a global phenomenon, and India a global destination for surrogate mothers.

India is quickly becoming the live destination for childless couples from all over the world. Until international surrogacy was outlawed in 2015, India was a popular destination for surrogacy because of the relatively low cost. Although no official figures are available, a 2012 United Nations report estimated that India had around 3,000 fertility clinics. Surrogacy in India is estimated to be worth $1 billion per year.

Because of the relatively low costs and easy access offered by Indian surrogacy agencies, Indian surrogates have become increasingly popular among intended parents in industrialised countries. Indian fertility treatment is roughly a third of the cost of the procedure in the UK and a fifth of the cost in the US, when flight tickets, medical procedures, and hotels were factored in. Surrogacy for foreign homosexual couples and single parents was outlawed in 2013. India's government outlawed commercial surrogacy in 2015.

To make the process even more smooth and transparent, many of the fertility assistance providers offer these services in a package, which is inclusive of the fertility treatment, transportation, charge of surrogacy or donation, and delivery of baby, etc.

CHAPTER SEVEN

THE NEXT DOOR

"Two roads diverged in a wood, and I – I took the one less traveled by"

~~Robert Frost

NATUROPATHY

Naturopathy, also called naturopathic medicine is a medical system that has evolved from a combination of traditional practices and health care approaches popular in Europe during the 19th century. It is a system of man building in harmony with the constructive principles of Nature on physical, mental, moral, and spiritual planes of living. It has great health promotive, disease preventive, and curative as well as restorative potential.

According to the manifesto of the British Naturopathic Association, "Naturopathy is a system of treatment which recognises the existence of the vital curative force within the body." It, therefore, advocates aiding the human system to remove the cause of disease i.e., toxins by expelling unwanted and unused matters from a human body for curing diseases. The goal of naturopathic medicine is to treat the whole person that means mind, body, and spirit. It also aims to heal the root causes of an illness not just stop the symptoms.

Naturopathy is a belief in the healing power of the human body, avoiding the use of surgery and conventional medicines. Many

Naturopaths in India now use modern diagnostic techniques in their practice. They reject the methods of evidence-based medicine and instead rely on alternative therapies and "natural" methods.

The main features of Naturopathy are:

1. All diseases, their causes, and treatment are one. Except for traumatic and environmental conditions, the cause of all diseases is one i.e., accumulation of morbid matter in the body. The treatment of all diseases is the elimination of morbid matter from the body.
2. Acute diseases are self-healing efforts of the body. Hence, they are our friends, not the enemy. Chronic diseases are the outcome of wrong treatment and suppression of acute diseases.
3. Nature is the greatest healer. The human body itself has the healing power to prevent itself from disease and regain health if unhealthy.
4. Naturopathy Cures Patients suffering from chronic ailments are also treated successfully in comparatively less time by Naturopathy.
5. Naturopathy treats all the aspects like physical, mental, social, and spiritual at the same time.
6. Naturopathy treats the body as a whole.
7. According to Naturopathy, "Food is only the Medicine", no external medications are used.
8. Performing prayer according to one's spiritual faith is an important part of treatment.

TYPES OF THERAPIES

Diet Therapy

According to this therapy, the food must be taken in natural form. Fresh seasonal fruits, fresh green leafy vegetables, and sprouts are excellent. These diets are broadly classified into three types;

- Eliminative Diet: Liquids-Lemon, Citric juices, Tender Coconut water, Vegetable soups, Buttermilk, Wheat Grass juices, etc.
- Soothing Diet: Fruits, Salads, Boiled/Steamed Vegetables, Sprouts, Vegetable chutney, etc.
- Constructive Diet: Wholesome flour, Unpolished rice, little pulses, Sprouts, Curd, etc

Fasting Therapy

Fasting is primarily the act of willingly abstaining from some or all food, drink, or both, for a period of time. The duration of the fast depends upon the age of the patient, the nature of the disease and amount and type of drugs previously used. Fasting can be with water, juices or raw vegetable juices. During fasting, the body burns up and excretes huge amounts of accumulated wastes.

Mud Therapy

Mud therapy is a very simple and effective treatment modality. The mud used for this should be clean and taken from 3 to 4 ft. depth from the surface of the ground. There should be no contamination of stone pieces or chemical manures etc. in the mud. Mud is one of five elements of nature having an immense impact on the body both in health and sickness. Advantages of using mud:

- Its black colour absorbs all the colours of the Sun and conveys them to the body.
- Mud retains moisture for a long time, when applied over the body part it causes cooling.
- Its shape and consistency can be changed easily by adding water.
- It is cheap and easily available.

Before using, mud should be dried, powdered, and sieved to separate stones, grass particles, and other impurities

HYDROTHERAPY

Hydrotherapy refers to using water as therapy in any form. For instance, it may act as a treatment for temporary skin-related issues, such as burns, or for chronic health conditions, such as arthritis and fibromyalgia. Water therapy uses either hot or cold water, with the water pressure and flow varying among treatments. The intention is to ease both physical and mental symptoms. Some hydrotherapy practices are as simple as sitting in a warm bath, which people can do at home. Other practices involve specialist locations or equipment, such as a cold sauna.

MASSAGE THERAPY

Massage is also a modality of Naturopathy and is quite essential for maintaining good health. Massage involves acting on and manipulating the body with pressure structured, unstructured, stationary, or moving tension, motion, or vibration, done manually or with mechanical aids. Massage is a substitute for exercise for those who cannot do the same. The effects of exercise can be derived from massage. Various oils are used as lubricants like mustard oil, sesame oil, coconut oil, olive oil, aroma oils, etc. which also have therapeutic effects.

There are seven fundamental modes of manipulation in massage and these are Touch, effleurage (stroking), friction (rubbing), petrissage (kneading), tapotement (percussion), vibration (shaking or trembling), and Joint movement. Movements vary according to disease condition and parts applied.

Acupressure

Acupressure is an ancient healing art that uses the fingers or any blunted objects to press key points called 'Acu Points' (Energy stored points) on the surface rhythmically on the skin to stimulate the body's natural self-curative abilities. When these points are pressed, they release muscular tension and promote the circulation of blood and the body's life force to aid healing. Acupressure can be effective in helping relieve headaches, eyestrain, sinus problems, neck pain, backaches, arthritis, muscle aches, and tension due to stress, ulcer pain, menstrual cramps, lower backaches, constipation, and indigestion, anxiety, insomnia. There are also great advantages to using acupressure as a way to balance the body and maintain good health.

Acupuncture

Acupuncture is the procedure of inserting and manipulating fine filiform needles into specific points on the body to relieve pain or for therapeutic purposes. According to traditional Chinese medical theory, acupuncture points are situated on meridians along which qi, the vital energy, flows. There is no known anatomical or histological basis for the existence of acupuncture points or meridians.

COLOUR THERAPY

Sun is the main source of light which has gifted seven colours i.e., Violet, Indigo, Blue, Green, Yellow, Orange & Red. The white colour is due to the presence of these colours & black is due to absence. Each colour has its specific wavelength which provides energy to the human body. Even ultraviolet ray has a drastic impact on an individual human body.

Air Therapy

Fresh air is most essential for good health. The advantage of air therapy can be achieved by means of Air bath. Everybody should take an air bath daily for 20 minutes or longer if possible. It is more advantageous when combined with morning cold rub and exercises. In this process, one should walk daily after removing the clothes or wearing light clothes at a lonely clean place where adequate fresh air is available.

Magnet Therapy

Magnet therapy is a clinical system in which human ailments are treated and cured through the application of magnets to the body of the patients. It is the simplest, cheapest, and entirely painless system of treatment with almost no side or after-effects. The only tool used is the magnet. Magnetic treatment is applied directly to the body parts by the therapeutic magnets available in different powers or as a general treatment to the body

HOMEOPATHY

Homeopathy, also known as homeopathy, is a pseudoscientific alternative medicine system. Samuel Hahnemann, a German physician, came up with the idea in 1796. Homeopaths believe that a substance that causes disease symptoms in healthy people can also cure similar symptoms in sick people; this doctrine is known as similia similibus curentur, or "like cures like." Remedies are homeopathic preparations that are made using homeopathic dilution. The chosen substance is diluted repeatedly until the final product is chemically indistinguishable from the diluent in this process. In many cases, not even a single molecule of the original substance will remain in the finished product.

Homeopathy is an international system with holistic concepts of treatment. The system is practiced in over 85 countries especially in Europe, Latin America, and Asia. In the United States, the homeopathic drug market is a multimillion-dollar industry. Homeopathic remedies are made from plant, animal products, minerals, or certain inert materials.

Homeopaths understand that the body, mind, and emotions are not independent and distinct, but are fully integrated into health, diseases, and treatment. Based on this holistic perspective, homeopaths use remedies prepared from natural sources that fit a patient's physical, mental, social, and spiritual aspects to stimulate the body's own healing powers. The public has tremendous faith towards Homeopathy for the treatment of acute and chronic health problems. Disease prevention and health promotion are its other strength.

India is a hub of homeopathy and India has the largest number of homeopathic practitioners in the world, who treats patient illness including their mind stress also solved. Homeopathic medicine is its safety and mild medicines which is a potent alternative to expensive medical practices in developing countries. All drugs are subject to a risk analysis where the benefits should outnumber the elements of risk.

Homeopath treat conditions ranging from headaches, fevers, stress, arthritis, maternal and paediatric problems, eczema, and so on. Homeopathic medicines are used as a standalone treatment or as an adjunct with medicines of other systems for a variety of clinical conditions. The main approach is diagnosis based on the complete history of the disease in the patient as well as on an understanding of the patient's temperament, personality, lifestyle and food habits.

The teaching and training in Homeopathy in India are identical with other medical systems. Registration with the State or Central Register of Homeopathy is essential to get legal protection to practice Homeopathy. For this one has to approach the Central/ State Council/ Board of Homeopathy.

Homeopathy uses animal, plant, mineral, and synthetic substances in its preparations, generally referring to them using Latin names. Examples include arsenicum album (arsenic oxide), natrum muriaticum (sodium chloride or table salt), Lachesis muta (the venom of the bushmaster snake), opium, and thyroidinum (thyroid hormone). Homeopaths say this is to ensure accuracy. In the USA the common name must be displayed, although the Latin one can also be present. Homeopathic pills are made from an inert substance (often sugars, typically lactose), upon which a drop of a liquid homeopathic preparation is placed and allowed to evaporate.

ACUPUNCTURE

Acupuncture is a traditional Chinese method used to relieve some health conditions and symptoms, such as pain. An acupuncturist inserts very thin steel needles into the patient's skin at multiple "acupoints." The needles rebalance the body's energy and prompt the body to release natural chemicals to fight the illness or symptom. It's a minimally invasive method to stimulate nerve-rich areas of the skin surface in order to influence tissues, glands, organs, and various functions of the body. Each acupuncture needle produces a tiny injury at the insertion site, and although it's slight enough to cause little to no discomfort, it's enough of a signal to let the body know it needs to respond. This response involves stimulation of the immune system, promoting circulation to the area, wound healing, and pain modulation. Contemporary research on acupuncture relies mainly on this theory.

When performed by appropriately trained practitioners using clean needle technique and single-use needles, acupuncture is generally safe. When administered properly, it has a low rate of mostly minor side effects. Accidents and infections do occur, however, and are associated with practitioner neglect, particularly in the application of sterile techniques.

Acupuncture can treat many types of health issues. Most often, people use it to relieve chronic (long-term) pain, such as Arthritis, Back pain, neck pain or muscle pain, Headaches and migraines, Knee pain, Menstrual cramps, Sports injuries.

THE PROCEDURE

Acupuncture points are situated in all areas of the body. Sometimes the appropriate points are far removed from the area of pain. The treatment involves,

Needle insertion

Acupuncture needles are inserted to various depths at strategic points on the body. The needles are very thin, so insertion usually causes little discomfort. People often don't feel them inserted at all. Between five and 20 needles are used in a typical treatment. It may feel a mild aching sensation when a needle reaches the correct depth.

Needle manipulation

A practitioner may gently move or twirl the needles after placement or apply heat or mild electrical pulses to the needles.

Needle removal

In most cases, the needles remain in place for 10 to 20 minutes while the patient can lie still and relax. There is usually no discomfort when the needles are removed.

KALARI AND MARAMCHIKILSA

KALARIPAYATTU

'Kalaripayattu' is a scientific heritage of Kerala and it inherits the technology of the body through which self, power, and behaviours develop in the right manner. `Kalarippayattu' is the martial art form of Kerala after a long setback during colonial rule. This treasure, inherited by present-day society, can be utilized for the development of Heritage Tourism in India. In Malayalam, Kalari means 'open space' and 'payattu' means to exercise in 'arms, practice'. Payattu means 'to become trained, accustomed and to practice'.

Kalaripayattu is known for its long-standing history within Indian martial arts. It is thought to be India's oldest surviving martial art, with a history dating back over 3,000 years. The Vadakkan Pattukal, a collection of ballads written about the Chekavar of Kerala's Malabar region, mentions Kalaripayattu. According to the Vadakkan Pattukal, the cardinal principle of Kalaripayattu was that knowledge of art is used to further worthy causes rather than to advance one's own selfish interests. Kalaripayattu is an ancient battlefield martial art (the word "Kalari" means "battlefield"), with weapons and combative techniques that are unique to India.

Kalaripayattu, like most Indian martial arts, incorporates Hindu rituals and philosophies. The art also bases medical treatments on concepts found in the Ayurveda, an ancient Indian medical text. Kalaripayattu practitioners have in-depth knowledge of pressure points on the human body as well as healing techniques that incorporate Ayurvedic and Yoga principles. Kalaripayattu is taught using the Indian guru-shishya system. Kalaripayattu differs from many other martial arts systems in that weapon-based techniques are taught first, followed by barehanded techniques.

Kalaripayattu includes strikes, kicks, grappling, present forms, weaponry, and healing methods. Because it was difficult to maintain flexibility and mobility while wearing heavy armour, Kalaripayattu warriors would wear very light and basic body armour. Warriors in Kerala belonged to all castes, unlike in other parts of India. Women in Keralite society received Kalaripayattu training as well, and continue to do so to this day. Keralite women such as Unniyarcha are mentioned in the Vadakkan Pattukal, a collection of ballads from Kerala, and are praised for their martial prowess.

STYLES

There are two major styles of traditional Kalaripayattu that are generally recognised and are based on the regions in which they are practiced. They are the Northern style, also known as Vadakkan Kalari, and the Southern-style, also known as Thekkan Kalari.

The northern style of Kalaripayattu, or Vadakkan Kalari, is primarily practiced in Kerala's Malabar region and is based on graceful and flexible movements, evasions, jumps, and weapon training. The southern style of Kalaripayattu, or Thekkan Kalari, is practiced primarily in Kerala's southern regions and specialises in hard, impact-based techniques with an emphasis on hand-to-hand combat and pressure point strikes. Internal and external concepts are used by both systems.

KALARI CHIKITSA/ KALARI UZHICHIL

Uzhichil or body massage is a staple in Ayurveda treatment but it gained popularity largely through the medium of Kalari chikitsa [treatment that is part of training in Kalaripayattu, the martial art of Kerala]. Three forms of massage are prevalent in the Kalari chikitsa system – enna thechu pidipikkal or oil massage, kai uzhichil or massage using hands, and chavitti uzhichil or massage using feet. In very rare instances, during training, students sustain injuries to their marmas [vital parts of the body]. They are instantly and completely cured, thanks to the intervention of the Kalari asans [masters] who are adept at giving the right treatment. That is because imparting and imbibing knowledge about the marmas is an important component of Kalaripayattu training.

MARMACHKILTSA

The word Marma is of Sanskrit origin 'Mrin Maranae'. The Sanskrit phrase, "mriyatae asmin iti marma" means 'there is the likelihood of death or serious damage to health when these points are inflicted. Hence, these areas are called marma. Marma in Sanskrit also means hidden or secret. By definition, a Marma point is a juncture on the body where two or more types of tissue meet, such as muscles, veins, ligaments, bones, or joints.

Marma therapy utilizes 107 points or "doorways" into the body and consciousness. The mind is considered as the 108th marma. Major marma points correspond to the seven chakras, or energy centers of the body, while minor points radiate out along the torso and limbs. These points range in size from one to six inches in diameter. The points were mapped out in detail centuries ago in the 'sushruta Samhita', a classic Ayurvedic text.

Marma therapy, a very light stimulation of points on the body is done. It removes blockages from the marma points giving physical and psychological relaxation and strength. This is a powerful process and a therapy that works with these subtle and sensitive energy points to open the energy channels in the body are called srothas. Marma points, when gently pressed on the skin can stimulate a chain of positive events.

Five Basic Catagories of Marma Points

1. Mamsa Marma(Muscles) 11 Points
2. Asthi Marma (Bones) 8Points
3. Snayu Marma (Tendons &ligamants)27Points
4. Sandhi Marma(Joints)20Points
5. Shira Marma(Nerves,Veins&Arteries)41Points

ROLE OF MARMA

There are four basic purposes of Marma:

1. It removes blocks in energy channels called shrotas.
2. It pacifies vata dosha, (air and space elements), bringing it to its normal path— especially vyana vata, (a sub-dosha which controls the autonomic nervous system.)
3. It creates physical, mental, and emotional flexibility. Because of ama (toxins) and because of vata, human beings after 35 or 40 years of age become rigid — and this happens to animals and plants as well. As vata increases in the body, it leads to degeneration. This rigidity means becoming fixed in ideas, emotions, and physical movements.
4. This gentle treatment creates an opportunity to experience powerful and dynamic transformation at the physical, mental, emotional, and spiritual levels by building a positive link with the unconscious mind. Many times, people are not able to go outside their 'comfort zone. They think they have absolute limitations. After Marma is done, they can start taking positive risks.

HOLISTIC TREATMENT

Holistic medicine is a type of healing that takes into account the entire person – body, mind, spirit, and emotions – in the pursuit of optimal health and wellness. According to the holistic medicine philosophy, the primary goal of holistic medicine practice is to achieve optimal health by achieving proper life balance.

Holistic medicine practitioners believe that the entire person is made up of interdependent parts and that if one part fails, the rest of the body suffers. As a result, if people have imbalances in their lives (physical, emotional, or spiritual), it can have a negative impact on their overall health.

In general, holistic medicine combines conventional medicine with complementary and alternative medicine (CAM) that have been scientifically proven to work. Yoga, Nutrition, exercise, homeopathy, acupuncture, and meditation are a few treatments that may be used together with conventional medicine as part of the holistic approach.

Holistic medicine is based on the following core principles:

- All people have an innate ability to heal and are responsible for their well-being.
- Health is a combination of physical, emotional, mental, spiritual, and social wellness.
- Treatment involves addressing the person as a whole rather than a specific illness.
- The goal of treatment is to fix the underlying cause of the disease or condition, instead of just treating symptoms.
- A person is not defined by their condition.
- Holistic practitioners work with the patient to understand the patient as a whole and provide appropriate treatment to them.
- Prevention is primary and treatment is secondary.
- Treatment outcome is determined by the relationship between a doctor and the person being treated.

YOGA

Yoga is an ancient physical and spiritual discipline and branch of philosophy that originated in India reportedly more than 5,000 years ago. Yoga is essentially a spiritual discipline based on an extremely subtle science that focuses on bringing harmony between mind and body. It is an art and science for healthy living. The word "Yoga" is derived from the Sanskrit root yuj meaning "to join", "to yoke" or "to unite".

According to Yogic scriptures, the practice of Yoga leads to the union of individual consciousness with universal consciousness. One who experiences this oneness of existence is said to be "in Yoga" and is termed as a yogi who has attained a state of freedom, referred to as Mukti, nirvāna, kaivalya, or moksha. "Yoga" also refers to an inner science comprising of a variety of methods through which human beings can achieve union between the body and mind to attain self-realization.

Yoga, being widely considered as an 'immortal cultural outcome' of Indus Saraswati Valley civilization – dating back to 2700 B.C., has proved itself catering to both material and spiritual upliftment of humanity.

There are six branches of yoga. Each branch represents a different focus and set of characteristics.They are,

Hatha yoga

This is the physical and mental branch that aims to prime the body and mind.

Raja yoga

This branch involves meditation and strict adherence to a series of disciplinary steps known as the eight limbs of yoga.

Karma yoga

This is a path of service that aims to create a future free from negativity and selfishness.

Bhakti yoga

This aims to establish the path of devotion, a positive way to channel emotions and cultivate acceptance and tolerance.

Jnana yoga

This branch of yoga is about wisdom, the path of the scholar, and developing the intellect through study.

Tantra yoga

This is the pathway of ritual, ceremony, or consummation of a relationship.

Yoga maintains that chakras are center points of energy, thoughts, feelings, and the physical body. According to yogic teachers, chakras determine how people experience reality through emotional reactions, desires or aversions, levels of confidence or fear, and even physical symptoms and effects.

When energy becomes blocked in a chakra, it triggers physical, mental, or emotional imbalances that manifest in symptoms such as anxiety, lethargy, or poor digestion.

Asanas are the many physical poses in yoga. People who practice yoga use asanas to free energy and stimulate an imbalanced chakra.

YOGA TOURISM

Yoga tourism is defined as travel with the express purpose of engaging in some form of yoga, whether spiritual or postural. The former is a type of spiritual tourism, whereas the latter is related to both spiritual and wellness tourism. Yoga tourists frequently travel to India to study yoga or to be trained and certified as yoga teachers at ashrams. Rishikesh and Mysore are two major yoga tourism destinations.

While India is the birthplace of yoga and a popular yoga tourism destination, yoga retreats and holidays are available in a variety of countries, with options ranging from simple stays in guesthouses and ashrams to 5-star comfort in luxury resorts.

Since the English rock band, the Beatles visited Rishikesh in 1968 to participate in a Transcendental Meditation training course at Maharishi Mahesh Yogi's ashram, India hasn't been a major destination for yoga tourism. The visit sparked widespread Western interest in Indian spirituality, prompting many Westerners to travel to India in search of "authentic" yoga in ashrams such as Mysore (for Ashtanga Yoga) and Rishikesh. This movement resulted in the establishment of numerous yoga schools that provide teacher training, as well as the promotion of India as a "yoga tourism hub" by the Indian Ministry of Tourism and the Ministry of AYUSH.

MEDITATION

Meditation is a technique for training attention and awareness, as well as achieving a mentally clear and emotionally calm and stable state, in which an individual uses a technique such as mindfulness, or focusing the mind on a specific object, thought, or activity to achieve a mentally clear and emotionally calm and stable state.

Meditation is used in a variety of religious traditions. Meditation (dhyana) is first recorded in the ancient Vedic texts known as the Vedas, and it is an important part of Hinduism and Buddhism's thoughtful stocks. Asian meditative techniques have spread to other cultures since the 19th century, where they have found use in non-spiritual contexts such as business and health.

Meditation has been shown to reduce stress, anxiety, depression, and pain while also improving peace, perception, self-concept, and overall well-being. Meditation's effects on health (psychological, neurological, and cardiovascular) and other areas are still being researched.

SIDDHA

Siddha medicine is one of the most ancient medical systems of India. Siddha is the mother medicine of ancient Tamils/Dravidians of peninsular South India. The word Siddha means established truth. The persons who were associated with establishing such a Siddha school of thought were known as Siddhars. They recorded their mystic findings in medicine, yoga, and astrology in Tamil. Fundamental Principles of Siddha include theories of Five Elements (Aimpootham), and Three Forces/Faults (Mukkuttram)

According to this system, the human body is a replica of the universe and so are the food and drugs irrespective of their origin. This system believes that all objects in the universe including the human body are composed of five basic elements namely, earth, water, fire, air, air, and sky.

As in Ayurveda, the Siddha system also considers the human body as a conglomeration of three humours, seven basic tissues, and the waste products of the body such as faces, urine, and sweat. Food is considered to be the basic building material of the human body which gets processed into humours, body tissues, and waste products. The equilibrium of humours is considered as health and its disturbance or imbalance leads to disease or sickness. This system also deals with the concept of salvation in life. The exponents of this system consider the achievement of this state is possible by medicines and meditation.

UNANI

The Unani System of Medicine has a long and impressive record in India. It was introduced in India by the Arabs and Persians sometime around the eleventh century. Today, India is one of the leading countries in so far as the practice of Unani medicine is concerned. It has the largest number of Unani educational, research, and health care institutions.

As the name indicates, the Unani system originated in Greece. The foundation of the Unani system was laid by Hippocrates. The system owes its present form to the Arabs who not only saved much of the Greek literature by rendering it into Arabic but also enriched the medicine of their day with their own contributions. In this process, they made extensive use of the science of Physics, Chemistry, Botany, Anatomy, Physiology, Pathology, Therapeutics, and Surgery.

According to Unani medicine, the management of any disease depends upon the diagnosis of the disease. Proper diagnosis depends upon observation of the patient's symptoms and temperament.

Unani, like Ayurveda, is based on the theory of the presence of the elements in the human body. According to followers of Unani medicine, these elements are present in fluids and their balance leads to health and their imbalance leads to illness.

Treatment includes regimental therapy known as Ilaj-Bil-Tadbeer. These therapies include cupping, aromatherapy, bloodletting, bathing, exercise, and dalak (massaging the body). It may also involve the prescription of Unani drugs or surgery.

CHAPTER EIGHT

AYURVEDA- THE ALL-SCHOOL REMEDIES

"No place is ever as bad as they tell you it's going to be."

– Chuck Thompson

AYURVEDA

Ayurveda, a natural system of medicine, originated in India more than 3,000 years ago. The term Ayurveda is derived from the Sanskrit words Ayur (life) and Veda (science or knowledge).

The philosophy of Ayurveda takes a holistic view of health, emphasising a balanced diet; physical fitness, healthy lifestyle, hygiene, and body care for a disease-free, long and healthy life. Ayurveda is based on the idea that disease is due to an imbalance or stress in a person's consciousness, and rejuvenates the vital organs of the human body. Ayurveda focuses on the therapeutic and rejuvenating aspects.

A notable trend in global tourism has been the popularity of health care holidays. The tourism industry has been responsive and is making effort to cater to this ever-growing market based on Ayurvedic therapy. Health tourism based on Ayurvedic therapy is popular in the south Indian state of Kerala.

The growth of Ayurveda was made systematic due to the existence of two great Universities in India, which taught various subjects along with Ayurveda in detail. One was 'Kashi' and the other one was 'Taxila'. According to mythology, Hindu Lord Brahma compose Ayurveda and divided it into eight branches they are;

- *Kaya chikitsa :- General Medicine*

- *Bala chikitsa :- Paediatrics and Gynaecology*

- *Graha chikitsa :- psychiatry*

- *Salakya chikitsa :- ENT*

- *Salya chiktsa :- surgery*

- *Agada tantra:- Toxicology*

- *Rasayana tantra:- Rejuvenation*

- *Vajikarma tantra:- Aphrodisiac treatment (for enhancing sexual vitality and efficiency)*

BASIC PRINCIPLES IN AYURVEDA

Ayurveda advocates the principle of disease rather than cure. The guiding motto of Ayurveda is "Jagathyeva manaushadam" meaning there is nothing without any medicinal value in the world. It relies on deep observation of nature functioning to understand the physical and nonphysical aspects of life. Ayurveda is a complete philosophy of life; it gives equal importance to the nonmaterial components of human lives like 'Manas' (the mind), 'Atma' (the soul), Indriyas (Senses), and Sharira (the body) and it focuses on maintaining a balance among them. Another important principle is Panchabhutas (the five-element theory), it states that the universe is composed of five basic elements they are 'Akash' (Space), 'Vayu' (Air), 'Agni' (Fire), 'Jala'(Water) and 'Prithvi' (Earth).

THERAPIES IN AYURVEDA

1. PANCHAKARMA

Panchakarma therapy is a preparatory procedure whose purpose is to prepare the body to discourage accumulated toxicity. It is a three-stage process, in which the Panchakarma treatment serves as the focal point. Some measures need to be taken before and after the Panchakarma therapy is applied, they are known as Purvakarma and Paschatkarma. Purvakarma is the preparatory procedure whose purpose is to prepare the body. This is undertaken before the actual Panchakarma therapy is administrated. Panchakarma starts with purvakarmas which includes deepana and pachana (use of digestives and appetizers), snehana (oleation,) and swedana karma (fomentation). After a few (usually three to seven) days of purvakarma the doshas are ready to be flushed out of the system by one or more of the panchakarma procedures. Pachatkarma, the final phase occurs after purvakarma and panchakarma.

Panchakarma procedures

The body normally uses three routes to eliminate waste products and toxins, the mouth, anus, and pores of the skin. panchakarma the foremost purification therapy reverses disease mechanisms by eliminating the toxic waste products and through these three routes. The procedures are as follows

Vamana krama (emesis)

Vamana means to expel the vitiated doshas through the oral route. This procedure is for discharging excess kapha. Vamana is always preceded by suitable purvakarmas in order to mobilize the doshas.

Virechana karma (purgation)

Virechana karma is for expelling the doshas through the anal passage. Virechana is the specific therapy for pitta dosha disorders. It purifies pitta function and consequently balances and strengthens all metabolic processes.

Vasti karma (enema)

Vasti karma is the most powerful of the five main procedures of panchakarmas. Vasti is the introduction of medicated liquids into the colon through the rectum, it cleans the colon as well as purifies toxins from all over the body. It restores the balance of the doshas.

Nasya or sirovirechana karma (head evacuation)

Nasya is a term applied for medicines or medicated oils administered through the nasal passage. Nasya karma is considered the best and the most specific procedure for diseases of the head. This procedure rejuvenates the tissues and organs of the head and neck.

Raktamokshama (blood Letting)

Raktamokshana, or bloodletting, it is an important part of the clinical therapeutic use of Panchakarma in the management of several important disease conditions. Raktamokshana is an effective blood purification therapy, in which carefully controlled removal of small quantities of impure blood is conducted to neutralise accumulated toxins.

when excess toxicity of rakta and pitta has occurred so much so that it cannot be cured by herbs or any other procedure, raktamokshan comes to the rescue.

Although Raktamokshana is the most limited of the five major procedures, it provides a rapid and sometimes dramatic reduction of symptoms in certain acute disorders where there is no time for the various phases of Panchakarma like Purvakarma (Preparation for Panchakarma), etc. Raktamokshana can be helpful.

KAYA KALPA CHIKITSA

Kaya Kalpa Chikitsa is a progeny of Ayurveda, a holistic approach to the science of healing. Kaya Kalpa has derived its name from the Sanskrit terms 'Kaya' means 'body' and 'Kalpa' means 'transformation' or 'transmutation'.

This secret healing technique is being used in India for thousands of years by religious healers to rejuvenate and give longevity to royalty and holy sages.

Kaya Kalpa treatments reverse the effects of time and regenerate the entire body, mind, and spirit. When the body is not in harmony, it causes distress, disease, and discomfort. Kaya Kalpa Therapy focuses on curing degenerative diseases and prolonging life by harmonizing the mind, body, and psyche through:

- Purification
- Nourishment
- Rejuvenation

The aim of Rejuvenation Therapy is to return youthfulness by rejuvenating each and every Dhatu or Tissue in the body and to maintain the normal level of Ojus.

Benefits of Kaya Kalpa/Rejuvenation Therapy

- Retards the aging process
- Improves immunity, vigour, and vitality
- Corrects metabolism
- Revitalizes body, mind, and soul
- Repairs worn out tissues
- Improves memory power & intelligence

- Relieves stress and strain

some of the procedures of Kaya Kalpa.

Abhyangam & Swedam

Ayurvedic traditional massage therapy Abhyanga is a whole-body massage therapy with specific herbal oils to nourish and revitalize the body tissues (Dhatus) and to allow the toxins to be removed from the body. Abhyanga has much deeper and far more reaching effects than an ordinary massage, that uses mineral oils and lotions. This massage is performed symmetrically by two therapists for one hour and is usually followed by a medicated steam bath (Sweda). It is one of the most rejuvenating treatments of Ayurveda.

Benefits: Increases tissue strength, improves blood circulation, rejuvenates the whole body, beautifies the skin, delays aging, induces sound sleep, promotes vitality, pacifies dosha imbalance, reduces stress, and removes toxins.

Shirodhara

Shirodhara is a classical and a well-established Ayurvedic procedure of slowly and steadily dripping medicated warm oil (Tailadhara) / herbal decoctions (Kwathadhara) / medicated milk (Ksheeradhara) / buttermilk (Thakradhara) / water or coconut water (Jaladhara), on the center of the forehead in an oscillating manner.

This procedure often induces a mental state similar to trance, which creates profound relaxation of the mind and body. It is deeply relaxing and revitalizes the central nervous system. Shirodhara gives the best results when taken after Abhyanga therapy.

Benefits: Shirodhara therapy is highly effective in anxiety, depression, stress, insomnia, epilepsy, migraine, hypertension, diabetic neuropathy, paralysis, hemiplegia, paraplegia, Strengthens the sensory organs, premature greying of hair & hair loss, mental retardation, ADHD, autism, cerebral palsy, Parkinson's disease, PSP, Alzheimer's disease, etc...

Thakradhara

Thakradhara is a form of ☐Shirodhara, involves pouring medicated buttermilk continuously on the forehead or the whole body in a rhythmic way. It is a very cooling, deeply moisturising, and relaxing therapy, done for 7 – 21 days. Thakradhara is highly beneficial in ☐Stress, ☐Insomnia, ☐Fatigue, ☐Psoriasis, ☐IBS, ☐Hairfall, ☐Graying of Hair, ☐Hypertension, etc.

Sarvangadhara (Pizhichil) or Kayaseka

Medicated oil/milk/decoction is poured onto the body in continuous streams while being gently massaged, for one hour. It is extremely soothing and relaxing. It acts as a free radical scavenger, toning, strengthening, and deeply rejuvenating the whole body. It is applied after Abhyanga.

Benefits: Increases ojus & body immunity, anti-aging & rejuvenating, alleviates the burning sensation in the body, ensures better blood circulation, helps to recover from paralysis, Promotes healing of fractures

Patra Pinda Sweda (Elakkizhi)

A highly rejuvenating treatment, in which fresh plants are fried with several other herbal ingredients and tied into boluses, dipped in warm medicated oil, and simultaneously massaged all over the body for one hour. It is applied after Abhyanga.

Benefits: Treats chronic back pain, loss of function of a part or whole limb, joint stiffness and swelling, muscular pain, anti-aging & rejuvenating, sciatica, spondylosis, sprains, and cramps

Sashtika Sali Pinda Sweda (Navarakizhi)

A highly effective rejuvenation technique using a special type of rice that is cooked, tied into boluses, and dipped into a herbal decoction and warm milk, then skillfully massaged simultaneously all over the body for one hour after the Abhyanga.

Benefits: Relief from paralytic strokes, anti-aging & rejuvenating, strengthens tissues, body ache, emaciation, debility monoplegia, osteoarthritis, rheumatoid arthritis.

Udvartana

This is a specialized herbal treatment for weight reduction. A herbal paste or powder is applied all over the body and deeply massaged with specific movements for one hour.

Benefits: Helps in toning the skin and muscles aids in obesity, weight reduction, imparts good complexion to skin, revitalizes the sense of touch, and removes Kapha, toxins from the body.

3. Kizhi in Ayurveda

Kizhi is a technique used in the management of various pain-related conditions affecting the musculoskeletal and neuromuscular systems. Kizhi is utilised in both Kalari Chikitsa and Ayurvedic treatments. It is often combined with massage to increase the pain-relieving benefits.

A Kizhi is a poultice that is densely packed with herbal ingredients and heated in warm herbal oil throughout the treatment. The Kizhi is massaged over the affected area or the whole body as required.

The warmth of the poultices, combined with the active ingredients of the herbs and oils, improves circulation and reduces body stiffness and pain. The Kizhi ingredients, herbalised oils, and massage techniques are all selected according to the type and cause of your pain.

Types of Kizhi

There are many varieties of Kizhi and the name is given based on the ingredients tied within the poultice. The kind of Kizhi used is chosen according to what is most suitable for your particular condition.

Marma Kizhi

This Kizhi is a specialty of Kalari Chikitsa and is included in the Kalari Marma Massage. As Kalari Chikitsa was developed to prevent and treat warrior's injuries, this Kizhi is useful in modern-day sports injuries.

The herbal ingredients in the Kizhi are made from secret recipes passed down through the generations from master to student. As with the herbal medicines and oils made in Kalari Chikitsa, each Kalari lineage has its own recipes.

Navara Kizhi (Shashtika Pinda Sweda)

The main ingredient in this Kizhi is Navara rice which is harvested in 60 days and is used exclusively for treatments in Ayurveda. The rice is cooked in a mixture of cow's milk and herbal decoctions and tied in a poultice. The poultice is dipped into warm milk and herbal decoctions throughout the treatment. The ingredients are rejuvenating and nourishing to the body.

Ela Kizhi (Patra Pinda Sweda)

This Kizhi contains fresh leaves of medicinal plants that are fried with other herbal ingredients. The Kizhi is then dipped into warm herbalised oil and applied to the affected body parts.

Naranga Kizhi (Jambeera Pinda Sweda)

The main ingredient in this Kizhi is lime which is cut and fried in herbal oil with herbal powders. The Kizhi is then dipped into warm herbalised oil and applied to the affected areas of the body.

Podi Kizhi (Choorna Pinda Sweda)

Unlike the other Kizhi varieties, this one can be applied with or without oil. The Kizhi contains herbs that have been dried and then pounded with a mortar and pestle into a fine powder. The Kizhi can be warmed in medicated oil throughout the massage or can be applied without oil when dry heat is required.

4. DHARA IN AYURVEDA

Dhara is a very ancient Ayurveda treatment system using mildly warm oil, and it's a method well known all over the world. There are many varieties of Dhara in Ayurveda and all the Dhara's are very result-oriented and ensure curing of ailments. Dhara is an important therapy in Ayurveda and it gives sudden relief from chronic headaches, insomnia, mental tension, hysteria, hallucination, and insanity, etc. Herbal oil, coconut water, milk, ghee, etc. are the contents for preparing Dhara. Dhara has the convenience to prepare with different materials and as per the change of such things, the name of the Dhara also changes. The main ingredient of every Dharas is medicated or herbal oil. It'll take 14 days to finish a Dhara treatment course. It's very amazing that Dhara gives a quick remedy to many health problems and its meaningful treatment system of Ayurveda, the treatment gets wide acceptance all over the world especially with westerners. Dhara treatment is 100% pure and natural and it plays a key role to uplift the dominance of Ayurveda to global access.

Shirodhara

Often called the 'third eye' treatment, Shirodhara involves creating warm herbal oil streams on the forehead, scalp, and hair. This treatment rejuvenates the body and mind by tranquilizing the entire nervous system. Very beneficial for Insomnia, sinusitis, depression, migraine, cervical disorders, Shirodhara proves to be an ideal tranquilizer.

Thakra Dhara

The Sanskrit word Thakra means buttermilk. Thus, in this therapy, medicated buttermilk is poured over the forehead. Results show an acute reduction in psoriasis, digestive problems, headaches, and graying of hair.

Ksheer Dhara

Best availed in the summer season, this form of Ayurvedic treatment involves pouring herbal oils or medicated milk over the head and body. Used to cure Vatha and Pittha disorders, Ksheer dhara brings relief in mental tensions, insomnia, headaches, and body aches.

Dhanyamla Dhara

It is an Ayurvedic massage therapy in which lukewarm medicinal liquid is poured on different parts of the body. Practiced for curing various types of spinal disorders, neurological disorders, arthritis, asthma, spondylosis, and more, this treatment is a sure shot formula for physical and mental well-being.

Sarvanga Dhara

Based on the internal body type of the patient, in this Ayurvedic treatment 6 to 7 liters of warm herbal oil is poured on the entire body. It is followed by a full body massage. Very effective in curing all types of degenerative disease, this therapy relieves you from muscular pains, joint stiffness, hormonal imbalances, and skin diseases.

Nethra Dhara

Done for rejuvenating eyes, the treatment involves washing eyes with Triphala water for cleaning the eyes plus removing different kinds of eye problems.

5. Nasyam

It is an ayurvedic treatment aimed at purifying the head region and nasal passages thereby eliminating Headaches, Migraine, and Sinus related disorders. The entry point of nasyam treatment is the nostrils which are considered as the doorway to the brain.

The patient is requested to lie down on a wooden cot placed in a warm room with their head placed slightly lower than the rest of the body. The head, neck, chest are massaged with medicated oils for relaxation. Then medicated oil is instilled into the nostrils alternately. The sole, shoulder, neck, and palm are gently massaged after that.

TYPES OF NASYA

Virechana nasayam

This method involves pouring down ghee or other herbal oil down the nasal passage to clear off toxins and eliminate them in the throat or head.

Pradhamana Nasyam

In this type of Nasyam treatment, dry powders, instead of oils are administered into the nose using a tube. It is effective in the treatment of conditions like sinusitis, hoarseness of voice, nasal congestion as well as chronic diseases like tumors and cervical lymph.

Snehana Nasyam

Also called Brihmana Nasyam, the Snehana Nasyam administers medicated oil mixed with camphor or other plant extracts into the nose. It works best for dry sinuses, dry nose, stiffness in the neck, bursitis, and loss of sense of smell.

Shamana Nasyam

This form of Nasya treatment uses milk, medicated oils, decoctions, and teas to treat disorders caused due to Pitta imbalance and vitiation of blood. It can prevent premature wrinkles, graying and thinning of hair, discoloration on the face, diseases of the eyes, etc.

Pratimarshya

The Pratimarshya form of Nasya treatment is an excellent therapy for opening up deep nasal tissues and relieving stress. It is suitable for individuals of any age and can be given in any season in the morning or evening. Pratimarshya therapy is generally performed after a head massage, oil pulling.

6. VASTHI

Vasthi is an ace among Ayurvedic Treatments. It is rendered in two ways: The first is by channelizing warm medicated oils or decoctions on the affected areas of the body through a concentrated channel made from herbal pastes or leather; the second is through a medicated enema. It is a highly effective treatment that helps treat multiple Dosha disorders, degenerative disorders, neurological ailments, rheumatic complaints, etc.

TYPES OF VASTHI

Kativasthi (Lower Back Vasthi)

A unique Kerala treatment where a frame of black gram paste is formed on the lower back and is filled with specially prepared warm herbal oil. This preparation is poured over the body after a massage. The powerful healing herbal oils deeply penetrate into the vertebrae, cleanse the blood and strengthen & lubricate the muscles, bones, tendons and ligaments. It is one of the best treatments for lower back ache.

Greevavasthi (Neck Vasthi)

Specially prepared warm herbal oil is poured over the neck and retained inside the black gram paste boundary for the required duration. The healing properties of herbal oils used for this therapy deeply penetrate, build and maintain the strength of the muscles and lubricate the cervical vertebrae keeping them flexible and pain free. Greevavasthi is highly recommended for conditions such as cervical spondylosis, stiff neck, neck and upper back pain.

Shirovasthi (Head Vasthi)

A leak-proof leather container is fixed on the head and prescribed herbal oil is retained inside the container for a particular duration. It is an effective therapy in treating most neurological conditions like facial paralysis, insomnia, headache, migraine, depression, etc. It also treats the dryness of nostrils, mouth, and throat.

Urovasthi (Chest Vasthi)

Like the other vasthis, warm medicated oil is poured and retained over the chest region through a channel prepared by herbal paste for a specified period of time. It is one of the main treatments for cardiovascular and respiratory disorders and helps treat various ailments such as chest pain, heart diseases, asthma etc.

Kashayavasthi (Herbal Decoction Enema)

A combination of decoction, honey, oil, salt, and other herbal medicines are used for this enema. It is the main treatment for all Vata disorders. It helps in pacifying the Vata Dosha and restores its equilibrium. It also helps to some extent in maintaining the balance between all the three Doshas namely Vata, Pitta & Kapha; thereby maintaining a state of health.

Snehavasthi (Herbal Decoction Enema)

This is an oil enema that is very useful in lubricating the colon. It is also the main therapy for all Vata disorders such as constipation, neurological ailments, paralysis, flatulence, lower backache, gout, and rheumatic complaints.

7. RASAYANA

The Rasayana therapy is a clinical specialty for Ayurveda that helps nourish the whole body by strengthening the *Rasa Dhatu*, the essence of all food we take, and which the body assimilates. Rasayana therapy contains various methods of rejuvenation. To develop a barrier against stress and infection.

Rasayana therapy includes drugs, dietary regimens, and codes of conduct. The possible mechanisms of action of rasayana therapy are Antioxidant, Immunomodulatory, Anti-ageing, Nutritive, Anabolic, and Neuroprotective actions.

Classification of Rasayana

Dravaya Rasayana

This includes Ayurvedic herbs and foods which are useful for optimum functioning of the body and brain. There are four types of dravaya:

- Age-promoting Rasayanas: These herbs and diets provide stability to life, vitality, stamina, glow to the skin, sweetness to the voice, and virtually tend to enhance the life span of a person.
- Mental acuity enhancing Rasayanas: These rasayanas act as an effective brain tonic and may help in increasing intelligence and memory. They enhance the grasping, concentration, and retention power of an individual and help in fighting mental fatigue. Examples of these rasayanas include cow's milk and ghee, herbs like Brahmi, vacha, and shankhpushpi, and bhrama rasayana
- Eyesight promoting Rasayanas: These are beneficial for and may promote proper functioning of the eyes thereby aiding a clear vision.

These include Ayurvedic herbal formulations like aamalki rasayana.

- Disease combating Rasayanas: Here, specific rasayanas are given to the patients suffering from some particular disease. For example, bhallataka rasayana is used in diseases of skin, and pippali rasayana is for respiratory diseases.

Adravya Rasayana

Here, general rules of living and the natural regimen of seasons are to be followed. All benefits of rasayana therapy can only be achieved if these good conducts are practiced on a regular basis.

- Avoid anger
- Be Truthful, free from ego
- Avoid consumption of alcohol, indulgence in sex, and violence
- Period of awakening and sleep should be regular
- Practice self-control
- Consume milk and ghee regularly
- Respect elders and teachers
- Practice spirituality

8. LEHYAM

Lehyas or Lehyam is electuaries or jam-like medicines, sweetened using jaggery or sugar. Some of the popular Lehyas used in Ayurveda are:

- Chyavanaprasa is a popular lehya consumed to reduce fatigue, improve health and immunity, and revitalize the body.
- Agashtya Rasayana is administered during the treatment of tuberculosis and cough. It improves stamina, and complexion, and is effective against digestive ailments such as sprue and constipation.
- Chinchadi Lehya is an effective remedy for anemia (iron deficiency), hemorrhoids, jaundice, heartburn, and acidity issues.
- Ajamamsa Rasayana improves strength and stamina and is used to treat Vata imbalances.

- Aswagandhaadi Lehya rejuvenates the body and helps combat anxiety and stress.
- Brahma Rasayana builds immunity and neural strength and revitalizes the body.
- Chiruvilwadi Lehya helps remedy Vata and Kapha imbalances. It is highly effective in the treatment of hemorrhoids.
- Dashamoola Haritaki Rasayana helps in the treatment of persistent fever, anemia, liver issues, and rheumatic disorders.
- Narasimha Rasayana is a popular remedy for premature greying.

9. ARISHTAS

Arishtas (Arishtam) are Ayurvedic medicines prepared by boiling medicinal herbs in water and then fermenting the decoction. Some of the widely used arishtas are:

- Abhayarishta aids digestion and is recommended for curing constipation and hemorrhoids.
- Amrutharishta is used for treating persistent fever, malaria, and also indigestion.
- Ashokarishta is used for treating menstrual disorders.
- Ayaskrithy is recommended for patients suffering from diabetes and other related issues.
- Balarishta is an effective remedy for rheumatic disorders.
- Dasamoolarishta is given as a cure for general debilities, urinary disorders, gastric problems, nausea, taste loss, paleness, ascites (swelling caused by a build-up of fluids in the abdomen), tuberculosis, and severe cough.
- Jeerakarishta is administered to treat post-natal problems, cough, tuberculosis, aphonia (loss of voice), and dyspnoea (labored breathing).
- Kudajarishta is medicine for diarrhea with blood and mucus discharge and bleeding hemorrhoids.
- Vasarishta is prescribed for the treatment of asthma, dyspnoea, haematemesis (vomiting blood), and aphonia

CHAPTER NINE

LET'S SET THE BASE

"Your most unhappy customers are your greatest source of learning"

~~Bill Gates

PROFESSIONALIZATION OF TOURISM

Professionalization is a social process by which any trade or occupation transforms itself into a true "profession of the highest integrity and competence." The definition of what constitutes a profession is often contested. Professionalization tends to result in establishing acceptable qualifications, one or more professional associations to recommend best practices and to oversee the conduct of members of the profession, and some degree of demarcation of the qualified from unqualified amateurs (that is, professional certification). It is also likely to create "occupational closure", closing the profession to entry from outsiders, amateurs, and the unqualified.

The process of professionalization creates "a hierarchical divide between the knowledge-authorities in the professions. "This demarcation is often termed "occupational closure". Professions also have power, prestige, high income, high social status, and privileges; their participants quickly become an elite class of people, breaking off from the general public and occupying a higher social status.

The professionalisation process tends to establish group norms of conduct and qualification for members of a profession, as well as to insist that members of the profession achieve "conformity to the norm." and follow established procedures and any agreed code of conduct, which is policed by professional bodies, for "accreditation assures conformity to general expectations of the profession."

PROFESSIONALISATION IN TOURISM

professionalism as a normative value, with recognition of professionalism as an ideology and general consensus that it is multidimensional Definition of professionalism, captures two dimensions of professionalism, namely, altruism and a code of ethics, but this fails to take into account the interpersonal and intrapersonal aspects of professionalism. It also fails to incorporate the qualifying attributes of a body of knowledge as well as specialist skills and expertise which have been identified as key aspects of professionalism in tourism.

On professionalism in tourism is scarce, and has been open to different interpretations. Dimensions of professionalism with a view to justifying their inclusion in the conceptual model starting with the importance of altruism.

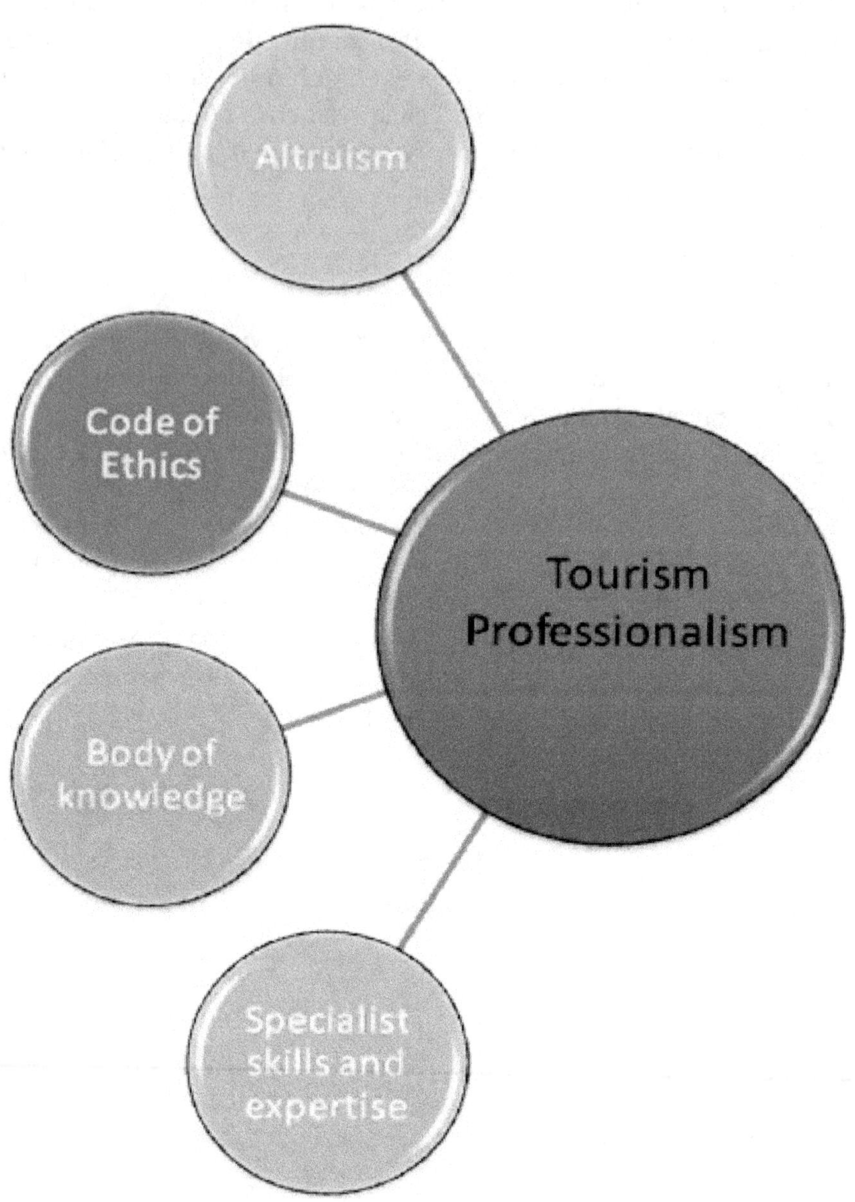

Altruism
Code of
Ethics
Body of
knowledge
Tourism
Professionalism
Specialist
skills and
expertise

ALTRUISM

Altruism is the principle and moral practice of caring about the happiness of other people or animals, resulting in higher material and spiritual quality of life. It is a traditional virtue in many cultures, as well as a central feature of many religious and secular worldviews. The object(s) of concern, on the other hand, differs across cultures and religions. Altruism may become synonymous with selflessness, which is the polar opposite of selfishness, in extreme cases. Altruism is the basis for some socially acceptable activities such as volunteering, charity, philanthropy, and blood donation. However altruistic behaviour, such as helping strangers, may expose individuals to risky social environments and attract criminals.

CODE OF ETHICS

A code of ethics is a guide of principles designed to help professionals conduct business honestly and with integrity. A code of ethics document may outline the mission and values of the business or organization, how professionals are supposed to approach problems, the ethical principles based on the organization's core values, and the standards to which the professional is held.

The Global Code of Ethics for Tourism (GCET) is a comprehensive set of principles whose purpose is to guide stakeholders in tourism development: central and local governments, local communities, the tourism industry, and its professionals, as well as visitors, international and domestic.

BODY OF KNOWLEDGE

A body of knowledge (BOK or BoK) is the complete set of concepts, terms, and activities that make up a professional domain, as defined by the relevant learned society or professional association. While the term body of knowledge is also used to describe the document that defines that knowledge – the body of knowledge itself is more than simply a collection of terms; a professional reading list; a library; a website or a collection of websites; a description of professional functions; or even a collection of information. It is the accepted ontology for a specific domain. In terms of the body of knowledge in tourism, tourism as a field of inquiry has developed over the past two decades.

SPECIALIST SKILL AND EXPERTISE

Skill is defined as "the learned ability to bring about predetermined results with maximum certainty, often with the minimum outlay of time, energy or both". The emphasis is placed on the fact that skill acquisition leads to predictable levels of task performance and accuracy in the case of professionals, the development of expertise. Professionalism has, since the times of apprenticeship in the nineteenth century, been associated with specialized skills and tourism education has traditionally been dominated by an emphasis on skill development.

STRATEGIC MANAGEMENT IN TOURISM

Strategic Management is understanding the management's aim and making a strategy to accomplish such aims by efficiently utilizing an organization's resources. It is mainly concerned with describing the management about its environment, developing strategies to comply with that environment, and assuming that the application of strategies takes place

In the frame of global tourism development, it is an indisputable need for strategic planning of tourism, i.e., the definition and existence of a development strategy for tourism, it is logical that its implementation is conditional on the functioning of strategic management in tourism. Strategic management is a proactive process of achieving long-term compatibility of the corresponding area in planned tourism. This management represents the most profitable way for the implementation of priority development goals in tourism.

characteristics of strategic management

- It promotes organizational efficiency in all entities involved in tourism. This means that the management imposes control through which it is perceived how successful one operation is running. Mainly the efficiency confirms whether the entities responsible for tourism development "perform things properly" because efficiency is determined by the relationships among all participants in tourism development.
- The support for strategic management and looking at the fact that it is always long-term oriented. Generally, as in tourism development strategy refers to achieving the goals that extend for a period longer than one-year, strategic operational management has the task to move all operations from the current position to the desired, future position. This means that the time horizon may be related to many years, decades, etc.
- It should be also emphasized, that the solely strategic operational management, speaks for the fact that it itself is based on decisions taken at the highest level, so-called strategic decisions. Such weight of decisions ensures authority in their implementation.
- Finally, another important aspect of strategic management, which should be applied if we want to achieve a dynamic development of the strategy in tourism, is that it could relate to different organizational levels, analogous to the definition and elaboration of development strategies in tourism: national level, regional level, local level, etc.
- If we define strategic management as the engine of tourism activity, there are several practical experiences in its implementation, regardless of the subjects that are affected by the development of tourism: domestic tourism entities or foreign investors who provide funds for tourism development. From the people's experience, whose job is to find suitable management personnel, for the necessities in the

area, specifically within the tourism industry, often there is a problem finding experienced managers for operational functions.

- The establishment of good managerial personnel in tourism means a team that knows well the mentality and habits of the local population, geographic and spatial capacities, tourism demand, competition, etc. Only good operational management can conduct the strategic and operational objectives set in tourism development.

The importance of strategic and operational management is important because, without successful operations parts, the development of the tourism component is threatened.

Benefits of Strategic Management

1. Alternative strategies

It helps the organization to opt for the best strategy options considering all possible pros and cons of the market environment.

2. Enhances employee's competence

It benefits the personnel of the organization to execute their duties with proficiency which serves to increase their efficiency.

3. SWOT analysis

It is a study by the organization to understand its strength, weakness, opportunities, and threats. It helps the trade to keep momentum with the dynamic essence of the environment stirring to the company. SWOT analysis comprises of four factors; they are as follows:

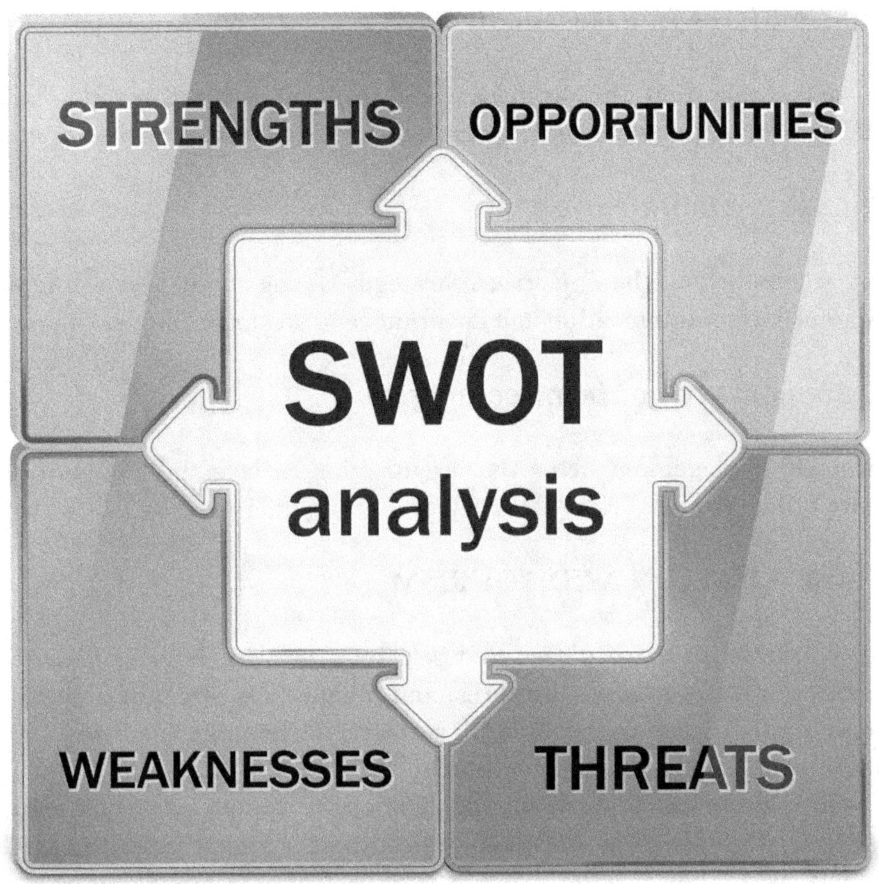

4. Benefits in planning

Strategic Management benefits the organization to construct economic planning.

5. Formulating Resources

Organizing adequate resources becomes possible only when the management has a systematic plan regarding what, where, and how the resources have to be utilized.

6. Stimulates in assessment

To make sure that the strategies and plans of the organization are effective and efficient; Strategic Management becomes a decisive aspect.

7. Ease communication

For accomplishing the objectives, Strategic Management needs to have appropriate communication and governance at all stages of operations.

8. Supports to confront competition

Strategic Management helps the organization to face the competition more productively.

GLOBALISATION AND TOURISM

Globalization is the word used to describe the growing interdependence of the world's economies, cultures, and populations, brought about by cross-border trade in goods and services, technology, and flows of investment, people, and information.

The wide-ranging effects of globalization are complex and politically charged. As with major technological advances, globalization benefits society as a whole, while harming certain groups. Understanding the relative costs and benefits can pave the way for alleviating problems while sustaining the wider payoffs.

Globalization plays important role in the growth and development of tourism on the world market. The process of globalization has contributed in a political, economic, and cultural sense, has directly affected the intensive growth of tourist travel. Increased mobility of people, the development of communication technologies, and the emergence of the Internet have contributed to the strengthening of international over domestic tourism. Also, global tourism trends indicate a dominant influence on the process of globalization and its reflection on the tourism business. All this clearly shows that tourism in the future will have to adapt to phenomena outside its borders and thus will undoubtedly be the most important and at the same time the most sensitive branch of current and future trends that affect the demand and supply of tourism products and services. Globalization is a kind of phenomenon that has contributed to the mutual connection between the countries of the world.

Globalization can also be simply described as the movement of goods, ideas, values, and people around the world. The term was first used in the early 1950s to recognize the increasing interdependence of economies and societies around the world. Globalization, however, has existed for centuries by way of evolving trade routes, including the slave trade, colonization, and immigration.

The Impact of Globalization on Tourism

1. Mobility and Travel Ease on a Global Scale

Transportation advancements that have enabled global mobility are especially significant. People can travel quickly and affordably using modern aircraft, cruise ships, trains, and other modes of transportation. By creating an aircraft capable of flying "long haul" distances with a smaller passenger load, aircraft like the Boeing 787 have opened up. People can travel, tour, and explore the world using fast trains, road systems, and even city bike rental programs. As a result of these changes, more people are able to travel more frequently in less time.

Ease of travel has helped overcome the barriers of fear, frustration, and expense. Multinational corporations have allowed for "one-stop shopping" for travel bookings. Mobile devices have also changed the nature of travel in terms of what travellers do and interact with a destination.

2. Free flow of information

Globalization has made it easy for travel enthusiasts to discover hidden travel destinations and to learn about different cultures before making their traveling decisions. There are more senior citizens in the developed countries today and due to the increased circulation of information, this non-working population is making more international trips than ever before.

3. Contribution to GDP and Employment

The contribution of the Travel and Tourism industry to the World's Gross Domestic Product and Employment is significant. Its multiple effects contribute to the world economy directly, indirectly, and through inducement activity of travel and tourism.

4. Terrorism, Safety, and Security

Terrorist attacks and political unrest around the world have slowed but not stopped tourism. Of course, the areas most affected are those where there has been unrest and which have received a lot of media attention. The Vision of Humanity organization's global terrorism index shows a fivefold increase in terrorist fatalities since 9/11. Many of the 18,000 terrorism-related deaths in 2013 were caused by groups such as the Islamic State (ISIS), Boko Haram, the Taliban, and al-Qaida, which represented a 60 percent increase over the previous year.

While safety and security may not be the primary factors in tourists choosing a destination, it is undeniable that a lack of safety and security will cause a location to be removed from travellers' "wish lists." As countries strive to protect their citizens, travel safety and security are becoming increasingly important. Government agencies all over the world issue advisories and warnings for a variety of reasons.

5. Increased Awareness of New Destinations

Another influence of globalization on tourism is a greater awareness of destinations and the range of leisure activities, sites, and cultures to visit around the world. Generating knowledge of a destination is obviously a key first step in marketing a destination, and this is achieved by way of travel shows, films, blogs, and other forms of communication. The competition to attract visitors is fierce considering the sheer number of places available for travel; it can be easy to get lost in the noise of global competition.

6. Poverty

Globalization has contributed to increased demand for goods and services and overall economic growth, with the result of global poverty has decreased over the years. However, at the same time, the gap between the richest and poorest has expanded. A significant portion of the world's population is simply unable to participate in, or benefit from, tourism. The economic gains from a tourism economy in a developing country such as India versus a developed country such as Canada are unequal. Simply put, not everyone has the same opportunities to profit. Environmental costs are also unevenly distributed in the world, with poor countries lacking the resources to adapt to impacts (such as droughts, increased disease, soil erosion), and shouldering the majority of the repercussions of phenomena such as global warming.

7. Tourism as a Force for Peace

In the 1980s, a popular hypothesis was that tourism supported global peace by allowing travellers to learn about other cultures and meet people from other nations. To date, there is little empirical evidence to support the claim that tourism fosters peace. Careful planning and policies supporting community well-being and sustainability are required.

8. Tourism as Cultural Homogenizer

Nevertheless, tourism does offer the opportunity to teach people about how to respect other cultures. Whereas some argue that globalization has a homogenizing effect on cultures, as Western values are spread through music, fashion, film, and food, rendering one culture indistinguishable from the next. But tourism cannot be viewed as the only means of transmitting western values. Some beliefs and values, such as embracing equality, inclusion, and diversity, or the need to protect children from harm, should be shared around the world. In the context of tourism and travel, these values are significant in the world of business and leisure.

9. CULTURAL COMMODIFICATION

Another possible influence of tourism on globalization is the process of cultural commodification, which refers to the drive toward putting a monetary value on every aspect of culture, from buying a sculpture stolen from an ancient temple to buying endangered objects such as ivory and coral or buying a T-shirt that desecrates a symbol or objects important to another culture. This trend results in the degradation or devaluing of cultural values and beliefs and was explored in Indigenous tourism.

TOURISM EDUCATION AND TRAINING

The tourism industry is rapidly growing and jobs in tourism management are becoming highly sought after. Working in this sector will offer a huge range of interesting roles, such as meeting new people and the opportunity to travel. Tourism management refers to everything that is related to the hospitality and travel industries. It offers extensive training opportunities for management positions in the travel, accommodations, and food industry. Tourism management can also include working in associations or agencies that are directly involved with tourism services.

Travel and tourism is an emerging sector that is rapidly growing and employing a large number of people, both skilled and unskilled, in today's world. This industry makes a significant contribution to India's GDP growth. The tourism industry's future is certainly exciting, but it is confronted with a number of human resource challenges.

The development and long-term viability of the tourism industry necessitate development strategies for tourism-related human resources and personnel, as well as the development of host communities and tourists. Work, culture, professional ethics, and operational practices based on sustainability are essential to tourism's long-term viability. Existing universities are now offering full-time tourism management courses. In comparison to previous generations, tourism education has advanced significantly.

INDIAN TOURISM EDUCATION SCENARIO

Tourism colleges in India offer a variety of courses in the field of tourism. The number of international and domestic flows is growing day by day. University Grants Commission has allotted Travel & Tourism courses at the undergraduate level in various forms like Bachelors of travel & tourism Management (B.T.T.M), Bachelors of Tourism Studies (B.T.S), B.B.A in Tourism & Hospitality Management etc. Also, there are a number of universities that provide MBAs in Tourism, MTA, and MTM, etc. Some private institutes are also running certificate, diploma & degree courses. Tourism education in India also received encouragement from the National Action Plan for Tourism announced in May 1992. Apart from the course on tourism management run by the I.T.T.M, there are colleges in universities of Gwalior, Kurusksetra, Aligarh Muslim University, Jodhpur, Pondicherry, and Indore that provide tourism education at the Master Degree and Postgraduate Diploma levels. The two important tourism activities are accommodation and hospitality; and travel and trade. Hence, the manpower development for the tourism industry cannot be confined to tourism education and training imparted by the national level institutes and universities only. With this objective in mind, the tourism planners in India both in the government and the private sectors have started Hotel Management, Catering, and Nutrition institutes.

SPREAD OF TOURISM EDUCATION IN INDIA

To cope up with the growing demand for trained manpower requirements to run the tourist offices, hotels, travel agencies, airlines effectively and efficiently; a carefully drawn tourism education plan has emerged as the primary need of the nation. Here are some of the strategies that can be adopted by educationists, tourist planners, private and government organizations.

- The study of tourism encompasses studies in the fields of history, culture, economics, psychology, sociology from the humanities stream, and on the other hand it includes studies in the fields of bio-science, environment, geography, and statistics of the science stream. Hence, tourism as an important subject should be introduced at the secondary and higher secondary levels in the Indian school curriculums.
- The young tourism bachelor's degree pass-outs must be required to have an on-the-job training program during their course and administrative training phase. This will enable them to have on-the-job exposure.
- The universities in the Eastern and Northeastern parts of the country should be provided required assistance by U.G.C., A.I.C.T.E. and

I.I.T.T.M to set up Departments of Tourism Administration
- Exchange programme with foreign institutes, both for the students as well as faculty.
- To bring guest faculties from international reputed tourism institutes. This would bring global perception to Indian institutes

Thus, some of these strategies suggested above will help in the maintenance of socio-cultural and environmental factors of the country along with the economic development of the nation through tourism

ROLE OF UNWTO IN PROMOTING TOURISM

The World Tourism Organization (UNWTO) is the United Nations agency responsible for the promotion of responsible, sustainable, and universally accessible tourism.

UNWTO's leadership vision acknowledges the most pressing challenges facing tourism and identifies the sector's ability to overcome them and to drive wider positive change, including the opportunities responsible tourism offers for the advancement of the 17 Sustainable Development Goals (SDGs).

UNWTO members have endorsed the management vision of the Secretary-General which seeks to position tourism as a policy priority, lead in knowledge creation, enhance the Organization's capacity through building new and stronger partnerships, and offer better value for existing Members while also expanding membership.

To realize the Management Vision, UNWTO's work is based around five distinct pillars:

1. making tourism smarter through celebrating innovation and leading the digital transformation of the sector;
2. making tourism more competitive at every level through promoting investment and promoting entrepreneurship;
3. creating more and better jobs and providing relevant training;
4. building resilience and promoting safe and seamless travel; and
5. harnessing tourism's unique potential to protect cultural and natural heritage and to support communities both economically and socially.

As the leading international organization in the field of tourism, UNWTO promotes tourism as a driver of economic growth, inclusive development, and environmental sustainability and offers leadership and support to the sector in advancing knowledge and tourism policies worldwide.

UNWTO encourages the implementation of the Global Code of Ethics for Tourism, to maximize tourism's socio-economic contribution while minimizing its possible negative impacts, and is committed to promoting tourism as an instrument in achieving the Sustainable Development Goals (SDGs), geared towards reducing poverty and fostering sustainable development worldwide.

UNWTO generates market knowledge, promotes competitive and sustainable tourism policies and instruments, fosters tourism education and training, and works to make tourism an effective tool for development through technical assistance projects in over 100 countries around the world.

UNWTO's membership includes 159 Member States, 6 Associate Members, and over 500 Affiliate Members representing the private sector, educational institutions, tourism associations, and local tourism authorities.

BENCHMARKING

Benchmarking is the practice of comparing business processes and performance metrics to industry bests and best practices from other companies. Dimensions typically measured are quality, time and cost.

According to Spendolini, 1992 "Benchmarking is a continuous systematic process for evaluating the products, services and work of organizations that are recognized as representing best practices for the purpose of organizational improvement."

DIFFERENT TYPES OF BENCHMARKING

1. Performance benchmarking

It involves gathering and comparing quantitative data (i.e., measures or key performance indicators). Performance benchmarking is usually the first step organizations take to identify performance gaps.

2. Practice benchmarking

It involves gathering and comparing qualitative information about how an activity is conducted through people, processes, and technology.

3. Internal benchmarking

It compares metrics (performance benchmarking) and/or practices (practice benchmarking) from different units, product lines, departments, programs, geographies, etc., within the organization.

4. External benchmarking

It compares metrics and/or practices of one organization to one or many others.

STEPS BENCHMARKING INVOLVE

• Stage 1 Planning

1. Select the subject area
   2. Define the process
   3. Identify potential partners
   4. Identify data sources and select appropriate collection method

• Stage 2 Analysis

5. Collect data and select partners
   6. Determine the gap compared to the benchmark
   7. Establish process differences
   8. Target future performance

• Stage 3 Action

9. Communicate to management and others

10. Adjust goal and develop an improvement plan

11. Implement

• *Stage 4 Review*

12. Review progress and calibrate

BENCHMARKING IN TOURISM

Benchmarking seems to be a suitable tool for all types of tourism organizations; however, its current use is often restricted to profit-oriented tourism businesses.In Tourism Benchmarking there are a substantial number of both conceptual and empirical attempts to formulate a benchmarking approach. Focus and methodologies used in benchmarking studies in tourism can be very different according to the application field. In principle, benchmarking in tourism can be classified into:

1. Benchmarking of profit-oriented tourism businesses

• Accommodation suppliers (Hotels, motels, bed and breakfast places, pensions, camping sites, etc.)
  • Restaurants (all forms)
  • Tour operators and travel agencies
  • Airlines
  • Other profit-oriented tourism service providers (e.g. amusement parks, diving schools, etc.)

2. Benchmarking of non-profit oriented tourism businesses/ organizations

• National or regional tourist boards/organizations
  • Attractions operated by public authorities or other forms of non-profit-oriented businesses (e.g. museums, galleries, theatres, operas, etc.)

3. Destination Benchmarking

• National benchmarking
  • Regional benchmarking

• Local (rural or urban) benchmarking

The overwhelming number of benchmarking initiatives can be found among profit-oriented tourism businesses, particularly in the hospitality sector. Benchmarking in all other tourism areas has been very limited in terms of number and technical quality.

BEAR THE RESPONSIBILITY

Good planets are hard to find – Let's take care of this one!

~~UNKNOWN

RESPONSIBLE TOURISM

Responsible Tourism is about "making better places for people to live in and better places for people to visit." Responsible Tourism requires that operators, hoteliers, governments, local people, and tourists take responsibility, take action to make tourism more sustainable.

Responsible Tourism was defined in Cape Town in 2002 alongside the World Summit on Sustainable Development. In Cape Town, the delegates from twenty countries around the world included people from all spheres related directly or indirectly to the tourism industry, right from tour operators, airlines, and hotel groups to national parks, government, and conservation authorities. They called upon all involved to develop guidelines to ensure the social, economic, and environmental protection of places where tourists visit.

The World Travel Market has adopted the Cape Town Declaration Defenition for its World Responsible Tourism Day which encourages the industry to take responsibility for making tourism more sustainable and demonstrate their responsibility.

The Cape Town Declaration recognises that Responsible Tourism takes a variety of forms, it is characterised by travel and tourism which:

- minimises negative economic, environmental, and social impacts;
- generates greater economic benefits for local people and enhances the well-being of host communities, improves working conditions and access to the industry;
- involves local people in decisions that affect their lives and life changes;
- makes positive contributions to the conservation of natural and cultural heritage, to the maintenance of the world's diversity;
- provides more enjoyable experiences for tourists through more meaningful connections with local people, and a greater understanding of local cultural, social, and environmental issues;
- provide access for people with disabilities and the disadvantaged;
- is culturally sensitive, engenders respect between tourists and hosts, and builds local pride and confidence.

Behaviour can be more or less responsible and what is responsible in a particular place depends upon environment and culture.

RESPONSIBLE TOURISM IN INDIA

Responsible tourism in India is becoming an increasingly popular mode of travel. 'THE RESPONSIBLE TOURISM SOCIETY OF INDIA' RTSOI/ ESOI works closely with the central and state government bodies responsible for sustainable tourism and a network of like-minded regional / state players across the country to facilitate and support the synergy of policies, initiatives, and activities at the national and state level. Formed in 2008, at the behest of the Ministry of Tourism, Govt of India, the founding members of Ecotourism Society of India comprised of 13 widely experienced, eco-sensitive professionals from the Tourism industry, state government departments of tourism and forests, wildlife conservation, NGOs and also Members of Parliament. This national body for ecotourism stood on three pillars:

-

Engaging in advocacy

- *Helping create policies and guidelines*

- *Helping with certification*

ESOI stood for Responsible and Sustainable practices In the Business of Tourism- and advocated our Collective Responsibility to ensure the Sustainability of the supporting Natural Environment and the Socio-Cultural surroundings for the Business to sustain over a long time. To highlight the above aspects, society has been re-christened.

The society is open for membership to conscious companies and individuals who wish to walk the Sustainable path and lend support to the cause.

RESPONSIBLE TRAVELLER GUIDELINES

On World Tourism Day, 27 September 2020, some guidelines have been launched by the Responsible Tourism Society of India and supported by the Ministry of Tourism, Government of India. Travellers need to be caretakers of this planet and the way forward is to be RESPONSIBLE! Tourism is a powerful tool and while both the Tourism Industry and the Government are working towards policies to make tourism sustainable, and urge the traveller to join hands in this endeavour.

Guidelines have been put together by the Responsible Tourism Society of India. It was established by senior and committed industry professionals, government officials, environmentalists, and a parliamentarian in 2008. RTSOI is supported by a range of stakeholders across the travel and tourism fraternity and multiple walks of life.

Planning your Holiday

- Give preference for a Responsible Travel Company
- Give preference to Hotels with Responsible Practices

At the Destination

- Bring your supplies
- Dispose of your waste Responsibly
- Eat local
- Cut Down on Waste and Conserve
- Shop Local
- Protect your planet
- Leave No Trace
- Animal Welfare
- Respect Cultures
- Support a Local Community
- Understand Local Laws

RESPONSIBLE TOURISM IN KERALA

Kerala, situated in the southern part of Peninsular India, is widely known for its salubrious climate, backwaters, Ayurveda, splendid beaches as well as rich history and heritage. The abundant natural and cultural wealth, along with its educated and hospitable people, forms the basis of the State's vibrant tourism industry. Realising the tremendous potential of tourism, the development paradigms, and the need for promoting it along sustainable lines, an action programme for practicing Responsible Tourism (RT) was developed in 2007 involving elected representatives, NGOs, policymakers, industry practitioners, community leaders, social activists, environmentalists, media persons, academicians, and other tourism stakeholders. It was decided to practice RT by giving due weightage to social, economic, and environmental aspects, with the cooperation and support of all the stakeholders in the tourism business.

Kerala initiated Responsible Tourism in February 2007 with the State level consultative meeting titled 'Better Together'. The State Level Responsible Tourism Committee (SLRTC) became responsible for planning and executing the RT programmes through the Department of Tourism (DoT) and the Destination Level Responsible Tourism Committees (DLRTC) planned and executed destination level programmes under the control of SLRTC.

First Phase

2008 – 2010 June

The Responsible Tourism initiative was implemented on a pilot basis in four destinations across the State, covering diverse geographical regions namely; Kovalam (beach), Kumarakom (Backwaters), Thekkady (Wildlife), and Wayanad (Hill station). The action plan for practicing RT was developed in a participatory framework and implemented through a consultative process, keeping in consideration the basic tenets of the Global Sustainable Tourism Council Criteria. The preparatory stage of the first phase involved scientific assessment of the daily requirements of hotels, resorts, accommodation establishments, and other service providers in tourism. Concurrently, a tourism resource mapping of the locality was done to identify areas where the community can get suitably involved in the tourism business. This was followed by a sensitisation programme for the local community and industry to accept and practice RT in the larger interest of the society, tourists and tourism business. By initiating a participatory approach in tourism, RT was able to create better places for people to live in and visit.

Second Phase

2011 – 2017

In Kumarakom, the second phase of Responsible Tourism was launched in March 2012. The four destinations chosen in the first phase successfully continued their journey in the second phase, and three additional destinations were added to this phase. Kumbalangi in Ernakulam, Ambalavayal in Wayanad, and Bekal in Kasaragod were the destinations. The destinations functioned as separate business units.

From February 2011, RT cells were placed at all destinations to facilitate the start of RT activities, which were facilitated by KITTS. RT focuses on promoting environmentally friendly and socially responsible tourism, as well as assisting travellers, local residents, and traders in gaining significant benefits from tourism. In the second phase, around 50 more destinations were chosen based on the first phase's overwhelming success. Under the broad heading "God's Own Country, People's Own Tourism," the government has decided to expand the programme to 112 Local Self Government areas. But project RT functioned as a parallel system without much connection to the official working of the Department at the state and district level and later the government decided to form a Responsible Tourism Mission for expanding RT activities all over Kerala.

Third Phase

RT Mission october 2017

The Responsible Tourism Mission has been launched by the Chief Minister of Kerala, Mr. Pinarayi Vijayan. Aimed at the development of local communities and growth of tourism in the State. The main aims of the mission are to eradicate poverty and give emphasis to women's empowerment. The mission aspires to provide an additional income and a better livelihood to farmers, traditional artisans, and marginalised people. Around 50,000 local residents will get trained in several activities and productions. The DoT hopes to provide direct employment to around 1,00,000 people in the tourism sector along with the support of RT Mission.

Around 20 Village Life Packages will be introduced soon as part of the RT Mission, taking tourists on a tour of Kerala's traditional handicraft productions such as coir, handloom, and pottery. RT aims to provide more benefits to the local community by incorporating traditional art forms, rituals, and handicrafts into tourism.

The RT Mission was formed with the objective of developing tourism with more popular, sustainable, and responsible tourism techniques. Within 5 years, 1,00,000 people will get employment in agriculture, production, sale, trade of traditional products, production and distribution of handicrafts and souvenirs.

Kerala Tourism Policy has RT principles as its base. The activities of RT will now be completely handled by RT Mission. RT Mission was formed under the leadership of the Director 0f Tourism with well This can be done by taking the principle of RT to the entire field of tourism activities and motivating the tourism service providers to take up the RT principles in their businesses. The principles of the first phase have been applied to the entire State, defined functional autonomy, With the introduction of the Responsible Tourism Mission, 14 districts of Kerala became a part of it. This can be done by taking the principle of RT to the entire field of tourism activities and motivating the tourism service providers to take up the RT principles in their businesses. The principles of the first phase have been applied to the entire State.

RT DESTINATIONS IN KERALA

KUMARAKOM

Kumarakom welcomes backpackers with a beautiful combination of greenery and blue skies. A walk-through God's garden, Kumarakom's paddy fields, is both enlightening and humbling. Backwater cruises in Kumarakom offer a distinctive and ravishing experience. The State's backyard beverage-toddy fills one with warmth and wonder. This tepid mild alcoholic drink made from the fermented sap of the coconut palm tree is a unique brew.

Kumarakom is located on the banks of Vembanad Lake, the largest freshwater lake in Kerala. Kumarakom was declared as a Special Tourism Zone by the Government of Kerala in 2005. It is currently a major Responsible Tourism destination of the State. On 16th May 2007, the first destination level meeting was held and the Destination Level Responsible Tourism Committee (DLRTC) was formed. It was the Kumarakom Grama Panchayat that initiated the implementation of RT at Kumarakom.

The net fishing practice in Kerala is truly a delightful sight to behold. Savouring the tastes of marine and freshwater fishes like Karimeen, shrimp, prawns etc. draw one to the ethnic tastes of Kerala. The ultimate crafted Kumarakom offers you the opportunity to watch the making of coir and the way its magical textures and natural properties are given life. The process has been perfected to an art and is mastered and passed on through generations. A blend of myriad experiences, Kumarakom truly is heaven made on earth. The beauty of coconut palm weaving amuses the spectator in equal measure.

KOVALAM

Kerala is a year-round favourite destination in the world. Kovalam Beach embraces backpackers with its tranquil waters and half-moon shores. Enriched with various traditional and prestigious ingredients, Thiruvananthapuram assures a unique ethnic hangout spot.

Apart from the shimmering waves and the alluring shores, Kovalam bestows one with the best Village Life Experience too making it a perfect spot in which to implement Responsible Tourism.

The first meeting to prepare for the RT implementation at Kovalam was held on 8th May 2007. The geographical area of RT comprised Vizhinjam, Venganoor, and Kottukal Panchayats. One can also watch traditional ways of fishing and explore the livelihood of the fishermen as well. A voyage through the deep blue sea in a canoe is yet another enchanting experience to behold

VYTHIRI

Cloaked in the mystic charm of riveting woods and exotic wildlife, the serene and soothing Wayanad is one of the major tourist destinations in God's Own Country. In Wayanad, Responsible Tourism was first initiated in Vythiri village on 1st Sept 2008 almost six months after its launch in Kumarakom.

The Village Life Experience of Responsible Tourism in Wayanad offers to travel through the sleepy hamlet Nellarachal. The experience ranges from savouring native cuisines to the making of indigenous tribal percussion instruments and handicrafts. Apart from its scenic beauty, Wayanad holds much historical significance too. The place has born witness to several legendary battles. Among them, the most famous is the guerrilla warfare led by Pazhassi Raja, a warrior prince with the support of the Kurichia Tribal community of Wayanad.

The Responsible Tourism Mission conducted training for more than 1060 people in Vythiri. Around 18 units were formed which carry out sales worth around Rs.68 lakh per year. Get a chance to visit the spice plantations, tribal art centres, Bamboo Craft Village, and many other places as well.

The geographical area of Wayanad in southern India is vast and required multiple DLRTCs to represent tourist attractions like Pookot Lake, Edakkal caves, and Kuruva Dweep. The implementation area was initially limited to Vythiri cluster that included Kalpetta, Pozhuthana, and Meppadi Panchayats.

KOZHIKODE

Kozhikode is considered by many to be the crown jewel of Northern Kerala. Its tranquil beaches, mouth-watering cuisine, and intrinsic bonds with the fabled Zamorin dynasty make it an absolutely mesmerizing location to visit. It is here that Vasco-da-Gama first landed and the legendary Spice Route came into existence. The Responsible Tourism (RT) Mission here helps travellers explore the wide range of tourist destinations and activities on offer.

The charming hamlets of Kozhikode are eager to entertain you with tales of their history, culture, cuisine, and unique means of subsistence. Witness fishermen extruding lime shells or catching fish using traditional methods to get a first-hand look at the daily lives of villagers.

The RT initiative lets you meet the craftsmen and discover the secrets of their art. Join hands with the locals and let them guide you through the less explored rural landscapes. The villagers showcase you the weaving of coconut leaves, capturing crabs, and making of the golden fiber-coir. The subtle beauty of the backwaters and the vast stretch of mangroves are the other major attractions here. A laid-back cruise through these is a wonderful way to escape the rigors of urban life. Visit Kozhikode, and let your senses be overwhelmed with joy at its legendary charm.

BEKAL

The package 'Kasaragodan Experience' involves a visit to cashew processing units, coconut tree climbing, toddy tapping, net fishing in the sea, and a visit to the Bekal Fort. Tourists get a chance to experience clay pot making, palm leaf weaving, and screw-pine mat making. As part of the package, tourists can also watch the ritual artform Theyyam. Another notable package offered by RT in Kasaragod is the Valiyaparamba Package. The package takes one on a trip through the weaving society, handicraft making, fishing, coir making, and so forth.

In Bekal from August 2017, several meetings were held with the active participation of the Panchayat president and members, CDS chairperson, members of ADS, supply units, Village Life Experience units and Kudumbasree units.

Training was also conducted for paper bag and cloth bag making as well as pappad making. Bekal has three candle-making units and pappad, paper bag, and head umbrella-making units, RT Mission also decided to conduct awareness programmes in Kayyur Cheemeni Panchayat. Traditional artisans, local people, Kudumbasree, Panchayat members, and all other tourism stakeholders will take part in the programme.

ECONOMIC ENVIRONMENTAL AND SOCIAL RESPONSIBILITY OUTCOMES

Economic Outcomes

- Increased and more equitably distributed GDP production of conventional goods and services
- Innovation, access, and uptake of green technologies
- Increased production of unpriced ecosystem services or their reduction prevented
- Economic diversification

Environmental Outcomes

- Increased productivity and efficiency of natural resources use
- Reduced adverse environmental impacts and improved risk management
- Natural capital used within ecological limits
- Other types of capital increased through the use of non-renewable natural capital

Social Outcome

- Increased livelihood opportunities, income, and/or quality of life, notably of the poor
- Decent jobs that benefit poor people created and sustained
- Enhanced social, human, and knowledge capital
- Reduced inequality

METHODS TO PREVENT THE IMPACT OF TOURISM

Tourism brings both positive and negative impacts on tourist destinations.Economic, socio-cultural, and environmental dimensions are the traditional domains of tourism impacts.

·

Economic impacts

The economic effects of tourism include improved tax revenue and personal income, increased standards of living, and more employment opportunities. Tourism's economic contribution is felt in both direct and indirect ways, with direct economic impacts occurring when commodities such as lodging and entertainment, food and beverage services, and retail opportunities are sold. Direct tourism impacts are influenced by residents, visitors, businesses, and various levels of government (municipal to federal) spending in or near a given tourism area. The fact that direct economic impacts of tourism occur within a country's borders and are carried out by "residents and non-residents for business and leisure purposes" is a key component. Another way tourism has an indirect impact on a community is through induced spending, which is the re-circulation of a tourist dollar within a community.

·

Socio-cultural impacts

Sociocultural impacts are associated with interactions between people with different cultural backgrounds, attitudes and behaviours, and relationships to material goods. The pursuit of authenticity, or the desire to experience a different cultural setting in its natural setting, is an inherent aspect of tourism. Although cultural tourism offers opportunities for understanding and education, it also has serious consequences. It's not just the amount of tourism at work that matters, but also the types of social interactions that take place between the tourist and the host. At the local level, there are three broad effects:

- The commodification of culture: Commodification of culture refers to the use of cultural traditions and artifacts in order to sell and profit from the local economy. With the rise of tourism, authors argue that commodification is an inevitable
- demonstration effect: It was introduced to tourism when the researchers were looking into the effects of social influences from tourism on local communities. The demonstration effect argues that local inhabitants copy the behavioural patterns of tourists
- acculturation of another culture: Acculturation is the process of modifying an existing culture through borrowing from the more dominant cultures

-

Environmental impacts

Environmental impacts can have both direct including degradation of habitat, vegetation, air quality, bodies of water, the water table, wildlife, and changes in natural phenomena, and indirect, such as increased harvesting of natural resources to supply food, indirect air and water pollution (including from flights, transport and the manufacture of food and souvenirs for tourists). People's desire for more authentic and challenging experiences drives their travel destinations further away from the planet's few remaining pristine and natural environments. An increase in environmental stewardship awareness could be a positive outcome. The negative impact could result in the obliteration of the very experience that people are looking for. There are both proximal and distal impacts to the tourist destination, as well as direct and indirect impacts, immediate and long-term impacts. There are three types of impacts to consider: facility impacts, tourist activities, and transit efficiency.

Despite the importance of tourism from its positive impact is always on the economic aspect. On the other hand, there are always greater concerns about the negative impact of tourism. Several effective ways or measures in order to reduce the impact of tourism are:

- *Diversification of product range*

- *Reducing or restricting the number of tourists.*

- *Promote Ecotourism, Green tourism, sustainable tourism, etc.*

- *Implementation of strict Law.*

- *Reduce Creation of Carbon*

- *Support Local People & Businesses*

- *Refuse, Reuse, Reduce then Recycle*

CHAPTER ELEVEN

UNDER THE CLAUSE

"A traveler without observation is a bird without wings."

— Moslih Eddin Saadi

TOURISM LEGISLATION

The primary goal of tourism law is to create a regulatory framework for the correct use, development, and control of tourist activities, which is backed by the United Nations World Tourism Organization (UNWTO). Essentially, the existence of the legislation will aid in the preservation of cultural traditions as well as the conservation of natural resources, among other social, political, and economic benefits. Furthermore, passengers and other stakeholders might benefit from fundamental legal protection via transparent processes.

According to Ronald A. Kaiser (Travel and Tourism Law, 1994), tourism law creates and defines seven basic concepts:

1) Travel is a legal right,
   2) Reliable and safe transportation must be readily available,
   3) Safe and adequate accommodations must await the traveller,
   4) All travellers should have access to such accommodations,
   5) Travel and accommodation costs must be reasonable,

6) Regulation of the travel and tourism industry is necessary, and

7) Redressal mechanism for transgressions of rights and regulations is necessary.

INDIAN SCENARIO FOR TOURISM LEGISLATION

No Central Tourism Act or Tourism legislation has been formulated by the Government of India. However, the National Tourism Policy has been formulated in 2002 for the development and promotion of the tourism sector which also contains basic principles for safeguarding the interest of tourists and tourism agencies.

These principles include:

- Government-led, the private sector is driven and community welfare-oriented actions
- sustainability
- earmarking a section of State Police to act as Tourist Police

- Accordingly, the Ministry of Tourism has taken the following steps/ initiatives for safeguarding the interest of tourists and tourism agencies:

i) Adoption of code of conduct for Safe and Hon'ble Tourism.

ii) Grant of Central Financial Assistance to the State Governments of Rajasthan, Uttar Pradesh, and Andhra Pradesh for setting up of Tourist Facilitation and Security Organization (TFSO) on a pilot basis.

iii) Issue of Guidelines on Safety and Security of Tourists for State Governments/Union Territories and Tips for Travellers in September 2014.

iv) Formulation of a voluntary scheme for granting approval to hotel projects and classification of functioning hotels under the Star System from the point of view of their suitability for international tourists.

v) Formulation of a voluntary scheme of approving Travel Agents, Tour Operators, Adventure Tour Operators, and Tourist Transport

Operators to encourage quality, standard, and service in these categories.

vi) The launch of a 24x7 Toll-Free Multi-Lingual Tourist Helpline in 12 Languages including Hindi & English on the toll-free number 1800111363 or on a short code 1363 offering a "multi-lingual helpdesk" in the designated languages.

vii) Issue of advisory to State Governments/UT Administrations for creation of Tourist Police.

Besides the above, under the provision of the Consumer Protection Act, a consumer can make a complaint in any Consumer Court depending on the geographical and pecuniary jurisdiction, about any defective goods or deficient services which also include tourism services.

There are a variety of laws in India that are directly or indirectly related to tourism. Some of these areas are as follows:

1) Environment-related

- The Indian Forest Act
  - The Wildlife Protection Act
  - The Forest Conservation Act
  - The Air Prevention and Control of Pollution Act
  - The Environment Act
  - The National Environment Tribunal Act
  - Coastal Zone Regulations, etc.

2) Monuments

- The Ancient Monuments Act
  - Regulations made by the Archaeological Survey of India
  - Guidelines issued by the Ministry of Culture, etc.

3) Accommodation

• The Sarais Act
   • Department of Tourism Regulations for Categorisation of Hotels, etc.

4) Protection of Tourists and Health

• Indian Penal Code
   • Consumer Protection Act
   • Prevention of Food Adulteration Act, etc.

Similarly, the transportation system is governed by various laws, rules, and regulations. However, these laws and regulations vary state-wise. Few states like Jammu and Kashmir, Goa, and Himachal Pradesh have enacted tourism legislation for regulating and controlling the tourism industry. These acts carry provisions like registering tourism-related businesses with state tourism departments for tour operators, travel agencies, hotels and guest houses, etc. They also give approvals to tourist guides and in some cases, a tourist police force has also been introduced.

STANDARDS IN TOURIST SERVICE

Standards are a set of guidelines and definitions technically related to an identified area, sector, practice, item, etc. standards are published documents of established specifications and procedures. It contains the instructions for all aspects pertaining to the development, delivery, and use of products and services. Standards fuel the development and implementation of technologies that influence and transform the way one lives, work, and communicate.

The mechanism through which standards are awarded and further dictated are called 'Certifications 'and 'License'. The tourism industry has several certifications and licenses required for the operation, development, delivery, and use of tourism products. Some of them are:

HAACP(Hazard Analysis and Critical Control Points)

ISO

UNWTO CERTIFICATION

GREEN GLOBE CERTIFICATION

GLOBAL SUSTAINABLE TOURISM COUNCIL

TOURIST GUIDE

Tourist Guides act as ambassadors of the country, they are the first to meet and welcome tourists and they are often the last ones to bid farewell to them when they leave the country.

Various international organizations such as the World Federation of Tourist Guides Associations (WFTGA) define a tourist guide as the person who guides visitors in the language of their choice and interprets the cultural and natural heritage of an area, which person may possess an area-specific qualification. Such specifications are usually issued and/ or recognized by the appropriate authority.

A tourist guide is someone who points out the way and leads others on a trip or tour. Generally, a tourist guide will work at a specific location, city, or province. In some cases, guides qualify to guide throughout an entire country.

ACTIVITES OF A TOURIST GUDE

- Learning: Usually, tour guides possess substantial knowledge about a destination, time period, or activity. A guide may have a personal interest in the subject, but their employer might request they complete formal training to help them gather the information that may interest or benefit tourists.

- Greeting and welcoming guests: Regardless of how long the tour lasts, most guides strive to connect with their guests. They usually start with an introduction that involves welcoming everyone and announcing the beginning of the tour.
- Explaining safety procedures: If a guide is leading an expedition, traveling in an unsafe area, or guiding from a vehicle, they may take a moment to brief guests on any conditions they need to be aware of or the procedures they can take in the event of an emergency.
- Providing materials: Some tours contain learning materials like brochures, maps, and audio recordings. Others may require specialized gear or uniforms. Guides ensure everyone in the group has access to necessary supplies and may also be in charge of maintaining equipment after its use.
- Responding to guest needs: For the duration of the tour, guides may be responsible for the comfort and well-being of their guests. This can mean making necessary accommodations, responding to first-aid emergencies, and addressing guests' concerns. Similarly, tour guides may have to provide information on pricing, trip length, and the frequency of their tours.
- Guiding tourists: As the name implies, a major responsibility of working as a guide is leading groups and individuals on tours. This may require guides to have the route mapped out beforehand and for them to share interesting facts with their guests about the locations they pass along the way.
- Translating: Though not always a requirement, for guides working in a foreign country, it can be helpful to know the local language. Some tour guiding jobs may require guides to be bilingual so they can explain written communication, interact with locals, and communicate with a variety of customers.
- Scheduling: Some tours require guides to purchase tickets, make reservations and work within time constraints. It can be important for them to plan excursions in advance so they can expect any issues or special accommodations.

In India, it's mandatory to own the license approved by the Ministry of Tourism (India) to work officially as a tourist guide. The government provides the license to a regional level tour guide and also runs a Regional Level Guide Training Program (RLGTP). These programs and training sessions are conducted under the guidance of the Indian Institute of Tourism and Travel Management (IITTM) or other government recognized institutes

TOURIST POLICE

Today, tourism is one of the largest and dynamically developing sectors of external economic activities. Its high growth and development rates, considerable volumes of foreign currency inflows, infrastructure development, and introduction of new management and educational experience actively affect various sectors of the economy, which positively contribute to the social and economic development of the country as a whole.

Safety and security are vital for providing quality service in tourism. More than any other economic activity, the success or failure of a tourism destination depends on being able to provide a safe and secure environment for visitors. It is undeniable that the tourism industry has a right to defend itself as well as to have a legitimate expectation that the government will ensure safety and security. It is, therefore, in the industry's own interest to coordinate its efforts and co-operate fully with the other main partners, i.e., the government, law enforcement agencies, and the wider community. It must recognize that when the environment is safe, the visitor is also safe and that if the travel and tourism industry emphasize security it will have a good chance of surviving.

Safety and security considerations become paramount for the tourists during their travel, their stay, and their visit to top tourist destinations. Law and order being a state subject, the safety and security of tourists is primarily the responsibility of State Government/UT administrations. Some of the State Governments have deployed Tourist Police for the security and safety of the tourists from their existing Police setup. However, this is not a committed force and there is always a possibility of their re-deployment in case of other pressing law and order situations.

Tourist Police should be in the control of state government like general police. However, the Ministry of Tourism, Govt. of India can provide financial assistance to the state government for effective implementation of the scheme. Under the scheme, a pool of trained policemen would be made available to render policing service to the tourists and would control the crimes at the places of tourist interest. The rules of the district police of the concerned state shall be applicable to the Tourist Police unless the contrary appears from the content in this scheme.

Duties and Responsibilities of Tourist Police

The Tourist Police personnel shall be deployed in the major tourist attractions including monuments, entry and exit points i.e., airport, railway stations, and bus terminals; religious places, shopping areas, entertainment areas, etc. which are prone to overcrowding especially during tourist season. The following shall come under the purview of Tourist Police:

- The prevention of crime and the maintenance of law and order in the tourist destination.
- To obtain knowledge of the people addicted to the crime at tourist attractions and to maintain adequate supervision over them.
- To ensure that all cognizable crimes are reported and registered as well as the tourists are encouraged to give full information in this respect.
- Taking charge of the kiosks, which act as reporting points for tourists in case of any security breach or for availing any similar kind of services.
- Curbing the activities of touts, beggars, and hawkers of the concerned area.
- The entry of unauthorized people, beggars, and persons hawking articles for sale in the tourist areas shall be reported as and when it is required.
- Making the travel of the tourists hassle-free by immediate intervention in case of any mishap.
- Providing emotional support to the victims when they are cheated, their belongings are stolen, or whenever they fall prey to any other mischief or wrongdoing.
- Imparting information to the tourists about locations, transport systems, facilities in the destinations, legal information, information about authorized shopping centres, information regarding medical help in case of physical assault, etc.

- Every Tourist Police person should show civility to all tourists and advice where they can get appropriate transport, accommodation, and other services needed.
- The tourist police person should be able to intervene in the event of pickpocketing, eve-teasing, harassment.
- The Tourist Police person should also interfere in case the tourists are involved in drug trafficking and consumption.
- Sensitizing tourists regarding the law and order system in the state like rules related to accommodation, entry/exit rules, reporting at local police stations, special permits; security conditions at the destination; social and cultural taboos, and other local conditions
- Tourist police should assist tourists while dealing with foreign currency exchange and guide them to do the same in authorized exchange counters and banks.
- To deal with immigration issues and laisoning with Foreigners Regional Registration Offices (FRROs) at entry/exit points as and when it is required
- Restricting the entrance of unlicensed tourist guides and other unauthorized agencies into the destinations and places of tourist interest.
- In the case of beach destinations and water-based destinations, the tourist police should be provided with an aquatic wing to enhance the security of the tourists

TOURIST POLICE STATION

The tourist police station, located in Mattancherry, Kochi, Kerala is the first of its kind in the country which makes God's own country more tourist-friendly. The station offers various services and facilities to foreign travellers like clarifying their doubts on passport and visa; registering complaints and grievances on lost passports and expired visas; hiring taxis; booking for boating, etc. From here, tourists can obtain route maps and brochures of different tourist destinations in the State. Within the tourist police station premises, there is a Police Museum that exhibits police uniforms, combat weapons, and armory, arranged in chronological order right from the colonial period to the present day.

ROLE OF GOVERNMENT IN TOURISM

The Ministry of Tourism is the nodal agency for the development and promotion of tourism in the country, as well as the formulation of national policies and programs and the coordination of activities of various Central Government Agencies, State Governments/UTs, and the Private Sector. The union minister for Tourism and Ministers of State is in charge of the Ministry. The Secretary is the Ministry's administrative leader (Tourism). The Director-General of Tourism's office is in charge of providing executive direction for the implementation of various policies and programs. Directorate General of Tourism has a field formation of 20 offices within the country and has 8 offices abroad. The overseas offices are primarily responsible for tourism promotion and marketing in their respective areas and the field offices in India are responsible for providing information services to tourists and monitoring the progress of field projects

The Ministry of Tourism has a public sector undertaking, the India Tourism Development Corporation Limited, and the following autonomous institutions:

- Indian Institute of Tourism and Travel Management (IITTM) and National Institute of Water Sports (NIWS)
- National Council for Hotel Management and Catering Technology (NCHMCT) and the Institutes of Hotel Management.

Role and Functions of the Ministry of Tourism

The Ministry of Tourism functions as the nodal agency for the development of tourism in the country. It plays a crucial role in coordinating and supplementing the efforts of the State/Union Territory Governments, catalysing private investment, strengthening promotional and marketing efforts, and in providing trained manpower resources. The functions of the Ministry in this regard mainly consist of the following:

All Policy Matters, including:

- Development Policies.
- Incentives.
- External Assistance.

- Manpower Development.
- Promotion & Marketing.
- Investment Facilitation.

Planning & Co-ordination with other Ministries, Departments, State/UT Governments., Regulation:

- Standards.
- Guidelines

Infrastructure & Product Development.

- Guidelines

Human Resource Development

- Institutions.
- Setting Standards and Guidelines.

Publicity & Marketing:

- Policy.

- Strategies.
- Co-ordination.

Research, Analysis, Monitoring and Evaluation

International Co-operation and External Assistance

- International Bodies.
- Bilateral Agreements.
- External Assistance.
- Foreign Technical Collaboration

The Functions of the Directorate General of Tourism are as under:

Assistance in the formulation of policies by providing feedback from the field offices and Monitoring Plan Projects and assisting in the Plan formulation

Coordinating the activities of field offices and their supervision, Regulation:

- Approval and classification of hotels and restaurants.
- Approval of travel agents, Inbound tour operators, and tourist transport operators, etc.

Inspection & Quality Control

- Guide service
- Complaints and redressal.

Infrastructure Development:

- Release of incentives.
- Tourist facilitation and information.
- Field publicity, promotion & marketing.
- Hospitality programs.
- Conventions & conferences.

CHAPTER TWELVE

WINDS OF CHANGE

"Like all great travellers, I have seen more than I remember and remember more than I have seen."

~ Benjamin Disraeli

GASTRONOMY AND WINE TOURISM

As global tourism grows in popularity and competition between destinations heats up, uniquely local and regional intangible cultural heritage is becoming a more important deciding factor in attracting visitors.

Food and wine production are integral parts of many destinations' histories and identities and have become a key component of the country's brand image. Gastronomy and wine tourism represent an opportunity to revitalise and diversify tourism, promote local economic development, engage a wide range of professional sectors, and give the primary sector new uses. As a result, gastronomy and wine tourism help to promote and brand destinations, as well as maintain and preserve local traditions and diversity, as well as harness and reward authenticity.

Gastronomy tourism is defined by the UNWTO's Committee on Tourism and Competitiveness (CTC) as a type of tourism activity characterised by the visitor's experience with food and related products and activities while travelling. Gastronomy Tourism may include activities such as visiting local producers, attending food festivals, and taking cooking classes, in addition to authentic, traditional, and/or innovative culinary experiences.

Eno-tourism (Wine Tourism) is a sub-category of Gastronomy Tourism that involves visiting vineyards and wineries, tasting, consuming, and/or purchasing wine, often at or near the source.

BLESUIRE TOURISM

Bleisure travel is a term used to describe travel that combines elements of both business and leisure. It typically takes the form of business travellers extending the duration of their trip, in order to enjoy leisure activities, which may range from sightseeing and relaxation, through to hiking, visiting entertainment venues, or attending events

A trip comprised of both business and leisure components may also be known as a 'bizcation' and travel of this kind has possible advantages for business travellers, their employers, and those in the travel industry. The boundaries between work and personal time are disappearing, and bleisure travel seems like the perfect blend of those two.

For the traveller, the primary advantages are likely to be a boost in morale and a reduction in stress. Allowing bleisure travel may help a business by increasing the number of employees who are actually willing to go away on business trips, while the subsequent morale boost can result in improvements to productivity. Finally, for the travel industry, the rise of the bleisure tourist means visitors who are willing to stay longer and spend more money in the process.

STAYCATION

A staycation (a " is a combination of "stay" and "vacation"), also known as a holistay (a " is a combination of "holiday" and "stay"), is a period during which an individual or family stays at home and engages in leisure activities within a day's drive of their home without needing to stay overnight. The term has increasingly come to refer to domestic tourism in British English: vacationing in one's own country rather than travelling abroad.

Use of a backyard pool, visits to local parks and museums, and attendance at local festivals and amusement parks are all common staycation activities. Some staycationers prefer to adhere to a set of rules, such as establishing a start and end date, planning ahead of time, and avoiding routine, in order to simulate a traditional vacation.

MOUNTAIN TOURISM

Mountain tourism is a type of tourism that takes place in the mountains "Tourism is a type of activity that takes place in a defined and limited geographical space, such as hills or mountains, and has distinct characteristics and attributes that are unique to that landscape, topography, climate, biodiversity (flora and fauna), and the local community. It includes a wide range of outdoor recreational and sporting activities ".

Mountain tourism has a high potential to stimulate local economic growth and social change because of its complementarity with other economic activities, its contribution to GDP and job creation, and it's capacity to promote the dispersal of demand in time (fight seasonality) and along with a wider territory.

URBAN TOURISM

According to the United Nations World Tourism Organization (UNWTO), urban tourism is "a type of tourism activity that takes place in a metropolitan area and is defined by non-agricultural economic activities such as administration, manufacturing, trade, and services, as well as being transportation nodes. For leisure and business, urban/ city destinations offer a diverse range of cultural, architectural, technological, social, and natural experiences and products ".

Urban tourism can represent a driving force, to make cities and human settlements inclusive, safe, resilient, and sustainable. Tourism is intrinsically linked to how a city develops itself and provides more and better living conditions to its residents and visitors.

Fulfilling tourism's potential as a tool of sustainable and inclusive growth for cities requires a multi-stakeholder and multilevel approach based on close cooperation among tourism and non-tourism administrations at different levels, private sector, local communities, and tourists themselves. Likewise, the sustainable development and management of tourism in cities need to be integrated into the wider urban agenda.

POLAR TOURISM

Arctic and Antarctic polar regions have always attracted tourists. Polar tourism is a dynamically growing industry due to the efforts tour operators take to provide various attractions, destinations, and activities for their customers. Adventure tourists and common tourists who long for unique weather experiences, solitude, and view of wild life in its natural habitat opt for polar tourism.

LUXURY TOURISM

It mainly pertains to the rich business tourists, who strongly believe that time is of prime importance and they must pay to save time at any cost. Wealthy tourists are inclined to undergo unique experience such as staying at a private island, personal attention from the service providers and access to elite class attractions and amenities

CULINARY TOURISM

The tourists who like to receive local culinary experience, like to tour for this purpose. They attend food festivals, food competitions, visit local farms, vineries, and cheese manufacturing companies, interact with local community or cooks for special culinary experience

SPORTS TOURISM

Sports and Tourism are interconnected and mutually beneficial. Sports, whether professional, amateur, or recreational, necessitate a significant amount of travel to play and compete in various locations and countries. Major sporting events, such as the Olympic Games, football and rugby championships, have evolved into powerful tourism attractions in and of themselves, contributing significantly to the host destination's tourism image.

Sports tourism is one of the most rapidly growing segments of the tourism industry. Whether sports are the primary goal of travel or not, an increasing number of tourists are interested in participating in sports activities while on vacation. Sporting events of all sizes and types attract tourists as participants or spectators, and destinations try to differentiate themselves by adding local flavor to them in order to provide authentic local experiences. If successfully leveraged in terms of destination branding, infrastructure development, and other economic and social benefits, mega sporting events such as the Olympics and World Cups can be a catalyst for tourism development.

SHOPPING TOURISM

Shopping Tourism is becoming an increasingly relevant component of the tourism value chain. Shopping has converted into a determinant factor affecting destination choice, an important component of the overall travel experience and, in some cases the prime travel motivation. Destinations have thus an immense opportunity to leverage this new market trend by developing authentic and unique shopping experiences that add value to their touristic offer while reinforcing, and even, defining their tourism brand and positioning.

More importantly, shopping is one of the most popular forms of tourist spending, providing a significant source of revenue for national economies both directly and through a variety of interconnections with other sectors.

BRIC TOURISM

The four major developing countries namely Brazil, Russia, India, and China have a great potential for driving global economy through hospitality and tourism industry. These countries are important for both inbound and outbound tourism. Global tour operators are adapting their tourism businesses to exploit the huge market these countries provide.

OVER TOURISM TO ZERO TOURISM

Stay at home — three words that have grounded holiday plans the world over as the novel coronavirus pandemic rages. The multibillion-dollar tourism sector, a growth engine in many economies, stares at gigantic losses; thousands of its workers — from top executives to ticketing staff.

The World Health Organisation declared the novel coronavirus disease as a pandemic in March 2020. The outbreak of the novel coronavirus restricted global mobility as cities and countries started to impose complete lockdown to curtail the spread of the deadly virus. The restricted movement of people and transport worldwide resulted in a metamorphosis from over-tourism to zero tourism within a short period.

Overtourism is the perceived congestion or overcrowding from an excess of tourists, resulting in conflicts with locals. The World Tourism Organization (UNWTO) defines overtourism as "the impact of tourism on a destination, or parts thereof, that excessively influences perceived quality of life of citizens and/or quality of visitor experiences in a negative way".

The travel, tourism and hospitality industry was among the first sectors to be hit by the Covid-19 pandemic and the attendant closure of borders; and it will also take the longest time to revive.

As the world continues its recovery from COVID-19, tourism, one of the industries hardest hit by the pandemic, has the opportunity to set itself on a greener, more sustainable path. It is a question of revival, but also survival: the industry's continued viability as borders re-open depends on it becoming greener.

UNWTO issued a joint statement with WHO, the lead UN agency for the global response to COVID-19 calling for responsibility and heightened coordination to ensure that health measures are implemented ensuring safety and protecting livelihoods. Stay safe and travel responsibly by following these simple but effective guidelines.

Key policy priorities include:

- Restoring traveller confidence
- Supporting tourism businesses to adapt and survive
- Promoting domestic tourism and supporting the safe return of international tourism
- Providing clear information to travellers and businesses, and limiting uncertainty (to the extent possible)
- Evolving response measures to maintain capacity in the sector and address gaps in supports
- Strengthening co-operation within and between countries
- Building more resilient, sustainable tourism.

ANAGHA SATHEESAN T M

~~~~END~~~
~~~~

www.ingramcontent.com/pod-product-compliance
Lightning Source LLC
Chambersburg PA
CBHW052037150726
48002CB00002B/649